THE Rugby World Cup 2019 Book

Graeme Copas

THE
RUGBY
WORLD CUP
2019
BOOK

Foreword by
WILL
GREENWOOD

Everything You Need to Know About the Rugby World Cup

Meyer & Meyer Sport

British Library Cataloguing in Publication Data
A catalogue record for this book is available from the British Library

THE Rugby World Cup 2019 Book
Maidenhead: Meyer & Meyer Sport (UK) Ltd., 2019
ISBN: 978-1-78255-174-4

© 2019 by Meyer & Meyer Sport (UK) Ltd.
Aachen, Auckland, Beirut, Cairo, Cape Town, Dubai, Hägendorf, Hong Kong, Indianapolis,
Manila, New Delhi, Singapore, Sydney, Tehran, Vienna

Member of the World Sports Publishers' Association (WSPA) www.w-s-p-a.org
Printed by CPI - Clausen & Bosse, Leck
ISBN: 978-1-78255-174-4
Email: info@m-m-sports.com
www.thesportspublisher.com

CONTENTS

FOREWORD

I believe the 2019 Rugby World Cup in Japan will be a memorable occasion.

When I think of the Rugby World Cup, I think of Jonah Lomu scoring four tries against England in the 1995 semi-final, and of Joel Stransky's drop goal and Joost van der Westhuizen's defence in the final.

I think of Serge Blanco's try against Australia in 1987 and David Campese's over-the-shoulder flip to Tim Horan against New Zealand in 1991.

I think of Stephen Larkham dropping his first ever goal for Australia, from 50 yards in extra-time, during the semi-final against South Africa in 1999 and that crazy semi-final between New Zealand and France.

Considering it was basically designed on the back of a cigarette packet in around 1986, its spectacular how big an event the Rugby World Cup has become, and I love it, but not just because I was a player.

I'm a rugby anorak and a fan, someone who enjoys big events. It's extraordinary how this tournament has grown into the third biggest sporting event on the planet. For me, it's all about the Rugby World Cup.

We all enjoy the Six Nations Championship and the Rugby Championship, they are classic annual competitions, but the Rugby World Cup only comes around every four years. There are some wonderful players who have never lifted the Webb Ellis Cup and some teams who have been magnificent in between, but it's the Rugby World Cup which defines you.

I've been to all Rugby World Cups post 1995 and they are special events. From a personal perspective as a player, I was like a kid caught in the headlights in 1999, even though I was 27, and then fast forward four years to winning a tournament I never thought we'd lose.

It's the changing room after the final that I remember, rather than the tackles and everything, just a group of lads who believed they would win and who had an idea they would never play together again.

Then, as a fan, to be in Auckland when New Zealand won in 2011 after 24 years, but thinking they might lose with 15 minutes remaining, and leading the opening ceremony in England in 2015 and singing Sweet Caroline with a packed Twickenham – what memories.

I've never been to Japan, but I'm excited by the prospect. I'm looking forward to the bullet train, Kyoto, a three-day walking tour between the semi-final and final with my wife and experiencing a different culture in what I'm sure is an amazing country.

I hope that the Japan team performs well, but England proved in 2015 that the atmosphere of the tournament will not be adversely affected if the hosts fail to progress to the knockout phase. Supporters are quick to adopt a second nation and it does not detract from the spectacle.

I'm certain Japan 2019 will be memorable, and I hope you enjoy this festival of rugby as much I will.

–Will Greenwood MBE
2003 Rugby World Cup winner with England
Centre for the Leicester Tigers and Harlequins
Co-host of School of Hard Knocks
Columnist for the Daily Telegraph

INTRODUCTION

In September, Japan will welcome the rugby world to its shores for the ninth Rugby World Cup, and the first to be held in Asia.

It is expected to be a pivotal tournament in the 32-year history of this festival of rugby, one which will attempt to showcase the best of what the sport has to offer, both to the world and to Asia, a region where rugby is not part of the culture but a legacy of empire.

Every four years, the sport comes together to celebrate and entertain, to bring nations big and small into the sporting spotlight created by the third largest sporting competition in the world. This festival is the culmination of a four-year cycle which hopefully ends with the rugby family becoming closer and feeling better about itself.

For many players, this may be the high point of their career as few will earn a greater accolade than playing for their country at a World Cup. Those who go on to lift the trophy will secure themselves a special place in the history of the sport. However, the World Cup is not just an esoteric idea or a festival; it also has a mercenary purpose.

The Rugby World Cup generates the revenue for World Rugby, the sport's governing body, which helps to keep the international game alive and always ready for development and growth. More than 95 percent of revenue distributed by World Rugby is ploughed back into the sport through investments in high performance funding and development grants. Without the World Cup, rugby would be poorer in all senses of the word.

However, there was a time when most nations and those who ran the game, particularly in the Northern Hemisphere, were against the idea of a world competition, fearing it would endanger the amateur status of rugby and its core values. Those pessimists were proved partially correct as the first World Cup was in 1987, and the sport officially became professional in 1995.

For many, the game had to evolve and is now better than ever before, retaining many of its values of camaraderie, spirit and respect while generating revenue to spread these values. It will be hoped by those who love the game that those values will be evident in Japan and embraced by a whole new audience.

But we live in the present, and spectators will also be expecting high-octane entertainment, provided by the best players in the world all focused on winning every tackle, every set piece, every moment and every match, and all for a shot at lifting the Webb Ellis Cup in Yokohama on Saturday, November 2.

There is genuine excitement ahead of the World Cup in Japan as the sport breaks new ground and attempts to market itself to a new, younger audience across Asia. Expectations are of a thrilling sporting occasion played out in front of the unique physical and historical backdrop that is Japan. Spectators will be expecting to experience the culture and natural beauty of the country, which is made up of more than 6,000 islands, while demanding modern stadia fit for purpose, integrated transport systems and high-quality hotels, restaurants and entertainment. This amalgamation of east and west, modern and historical, vibrant and Zen, capitalist and spiritual is what Japan does best and could form the basis of the most remarkable World Cup ever.

However, it has a lot to live up to and reputations are on the line. World Rugby made the decision to grant host nation status to Japan as a way of expanding all aspects of the sport into a growth market, but it was still a huge risk. If the tournament suffers from practical or logistical issues, and ultimately fails to generate expected revenues, then those charged with running the world game will be scrutinised.

The country itself is also keen for the tournament to be a success for financial reasons – the World Cup could inject an excess of $3 billion into the country's economy – and, in part, lay a platform for when it hosts the 2020 Olympics. Positively, there has been more than 2.5 million ticket applications for the 1.8 million seats, of which 30 percent have come from outside of Japan. For all stakeholders, World Cups are the foundations of the sport, and this World Cup in particular is one which the rugby authorities want to build on to reach new heights.

As it has been since the mid-1980s, the story of the Rugby World Cup is the story of international rugby. I hope you enjoy reading this book and following this evolving story.

In writing this book, I have attempted to make the language straight forward enough for novices to the game, newsworthy enough for those with a passing interest, and detailed enough for die-hard rugby fans. Many thanks to those who have helped me in my career, allowing me to reach the point where I have been able to attempt such an undertaking, and also to 2003 World Cup winner Will Greenwood for the foreword to this book.

A glossary at the back of the book will help in understanding some of the technical aspects of the game, the laws, the rugby-speak, the organisations and the competitions which make up the game.

Compiling this book has been a learning experience, expanding my knowledge of a sport that I thought I understood, and of a country I knew little about. Having gone through this process, I have developed a much deeper understanding which I hope that you are also able to share after reading this book.

Enjoy the 2019 Rugby World Cup. I know I will.

(Note: All information, facts and figures in this book are correct up to and including April 15, 2019).

CHAPTER 1
RUGBY WORLD CUP HISTORY

INTERNATIONAL RUGBY BEFORE THE WORLD CUP

The Rugby World Cup may now be the jewel in the crown, the pinnacle of the sport, but that was not always the case.

The sport's governing body World Rugby, first known as the International Rugby Football Board (IRFB) and then the International Rugby Board (IRB), were initially opposed to the idea of a World Cup or any tournament featuring international teams. The IRFB was founded in 1886 by Scotland, Wales and Ireland with England joining the fold four years later.

In 1949, Australia, New Zealand and South Africa became full members, as did France in 1978. In 1969, the IRFB passed a motion banning countries from participating in tournaments or competitions comprised of several nations. The board declared that it would not give approval 'to participation by teams from member unions in any competition or tournament, at whatever level, or wherever taking place, in which teams from several countries take part.' They feared that change would alter the nature of what was still a worldwide amateur game, and so the IRFB remained firmly against the concept of a World Cup for the next 15 years.

However, over the years, the attitude of many of the member countries altered as the threat of rebel, unauthorised tournaments began to increase. The Southern Hemisphere teams were always more open to the idea and, unknown to each other, both New Zealand and Australia wrote to the IRFB in 1983 asking for permission to host a World Cup. The Kiwis were keen to grow the game and demonstrate their skill to a larger audience, while the Aussies were hoping to coincide the event with their country's bicentennial in 1988.

The catalyst for change proved to be Australian entrepreneur David Lord, who was attempting to arrange an unofficial tournament made up of the best international players and teams in the world. The idea grew in momentum due to the popularity and financial success of World Series Cricket, organised by fellow Aussie Kerry Packer. Numerous elite players secretly signed up with David Lord, eventually forcing the IRFB's hand.

Under pressure from this threat, and with the knowledge that it might lose control of the game at the highest level, the IRFB reluctantly commissioned a feasibility study in 1984 into holding a World Cup.

A year later, the eight members of the board – Australia, New Zealand, South Africa, England, France, Ireland, Wales and Scotland – voted 6-2 in favour of hosting a World Cup. Only Ireland and Scotland voted against, because they feared it would threaten the amateur nature of the game, while France voted yes but only with the condition of the tournament being open to some of the smaller rugby playing nations. Seven of the eight IRFB members were invited to take part in the inaugural World Cup. South Africa, which was run under the Apartheid system, did not compete because of the international sporting boycott in place at the time and were replaced by Zimbabwe.

To take the number of competitors up to 16, eight other countries were invited: Argentina, Canada, Romania, USSR, Japan, Fiji, Italy and Tonga. The USSR did not accept the offer, so their place was taken by the USA. It was agreed that the tournament would be jointly hosted by Australia and New Zealand in 1987. They would play for a silver gilt trophy, purchased for £6,000 from Garrards in London, and named the Webb Ellis Cup after the inventor of the sport William Webb Ellis. From this point onwards, the worldwide perception of the sport was to change forever.

Before 1987, the international schedule had been built around countries taking part in lengthy tours, plus the five senior teams from the Northern Hemisphere playing each other in the Five Nations tournament (latterly to become the Si x Nations with the addition of Italy in 2000). The decision to host a World Cup was literally a game-changer, and one which would forever shape the tone of the sport's growth.

The road to the first World Cup may have been built on a long, steep gradient, but it would eventually lead to what is now the showcase event for the sport, its players, coaches, officials and supporters.

The Rugby World Cup, held over the course of seven weeks, is now the third largest sporting tournament in the world, generating huge revenues and interest in the game.

World Rugby states that the commercial success of the World Cup 'drives' the global game, which now comprises more than 9 million players, and 338 million fans affiliated via 123 national member unions. The sports international governing body anticipates that it will invest £428 million back into the game for the 2016-19 period, a 38 percent increase on the previous four-year cycle, much of which will have been derived from the cash cow which is the Rugby World Cup.

Not bad for a tournament which many believed would change the game only for the worse.

AUSTRALIA AND NEW ZEALAND HOST THE 1987 RUGBY WORLD CUP

Joint hosts and favourites, New Zealand, were winners of the inaugural World Cup, overcoming France 29-9 in the final held at Eden Park, Auckland on June 20, 1987. Witnessed by a partisan, sell-out crowd of 48,000, the All Blacks were emphatic champions thanks to tries from skipper David Kirk, Michael Jones and John Kirwan, while Grant Fox maintained his form with the boot to kick 17 points.

Pierre Berbizier's late try was a mere consolation for France. The All Blacks underlined their claim to be the best in the world by being the first team to lift the Webb Ellis Cup. They remained unbeaten in the tournament, scoring 43 tries and conceding just 4.

Try-scorers Kirwan and Jones were two of the stars for the All Blacks during the tournament, but it was the metronomic kicking of fly-half Grant Fox which ensured that they were never seriously challenged. Fox notched 126 points with the boot in the All Blacks' six matches, a record which remains today.

The champions began the tournament with an impressive 70-6 victory over Italy in the opening match of the tournament, and they went on to comfortably win Pool 3 following successes over Fiji (74-13) and Argentina (46-15). Fiji were runners-up in the pool. Pool 1 was won by Australia, who set up their success with a morale-boosting 19-6 victory over England in Sydney.

David Campese and Simon Poidevin dotted down for the Wallabies while Michael Lynagh kicked the extras. Mike Harrison managed England's only try. Both teams followed up this contest with wins over Japan and the USA. Australia were joined in the last eight by runners-up England. Wales finished top of Pool 2, thanks to a tough, physical 13-6 win over Ireland who finished the pool stage in second place. Like most of the smaller nations in this inaugural World Cup, the other two sides in the pool, Canada and Tonga, struggled to make an impact on the senior teams.

Pool 4 was eventually claimed by France over runners-up Scotland, but only on points difference after the match between the two old adversaries had finished 20-20 – the first draw in World Cup history. Romania and Zimbabwe were the teams to be knocked out of Pool 4.

The quarter-finals began with New Zealand overwhelming Scotland 30-3, Alan Whetton and John Gallagher bagging tries for the hosts. Australia were also comfortable winners in the quarter-finals, scoring four tries in beating Ireland 33-15, while France matched this number of tries in their 31-16 triumph over Fiji. It was a solid win for Les Bleus, but in reaching the quarter-finals, the Fijians had won the hearts of rugby fans all over the world. The tightest tie of the last eight was between Wales and England in Brisbane, a match which saw Wales come through deserved 16-3 winners after tries from Gareth Roberts, Robert Jones and John Devereaux.

The semi-finals were a complete contrast to each other. In one of the best matches of the whole tournament, France narrowly beat Australia in Sydney 30-24, despite the Wallabies leading on three separate occasions. The shock result was clinched by enigmatic fullback Serge Blanco who produced a solo effort to score a late try for Les Bleus. The other semi was a more one-sided affair with the All Blacks running in eight tries in a 49-6 thumping of Wales in Brisbane. The inspirational Wayne 'Buck' Shelford scored twice for the Kiwis in the contest. The match will most likely be remembered for the sending-off of Huw Richards for throwing a punch at Gary Whetton, the Welsh second row becoming the first player to be dismissed at a World Cup.

Wales did, however, end their campaign on a high when they edged past Australia 22-21 in an exciting bronze medal final. The Wallabies had flanker David Codey sent off early, yet still led by five points heading into the final minutes. The result was decided by a late try from Adrian Hadley and a calm conversion from the touchline by Paul Thorburn. The All Blacks then overcame France 29-9 in the final to win the first Rugby World Cup.

The tournament had been a success – on and off the pitch – laying the groundwork for the money-spinning, crowd-pleasing tournaments which were to follow at four-year intervals. However, the genie was out of the bottle, the commercial success of the competition was there for all to see, particularly to the players who were still amateurs. The game had been changed forever.

Tournament stats:

Teams: 16

Matches: 32

Total attendance: 448,318

Leading points scorers: 126 - Grant Fox (NZ); 82 – Michael Lynagh (Aus); 62 – Gavin Hasting (Sco); 53 – Didier Camberabero (Fra); 43 – Jonathan Webb (Eng).

Leading try scorers: 6 – Craig Green (NZ), John Kirwan (NZ); 5 – Matt Burke (Aus), Mike Harrison (Eng), John Gallagher (NZ), Alan Whetton (NZ), David Kirk (NZ).

Gate receipts: £3.3 million

Global television audience: 300 million

ENGLAND HOSTS THE 1991 RUGBY WORLD CUP

The second Rugby World Cup was staged across five Northern Hemisphere countries – primarily England but also Ireland, Wales, Scotland and France – with the final being held at Twickenham in London. This showcase final saw Australia narrowly overcome hosts England 12-6 to ensure the return of the Webb Ellis Cup to the Southern Hemisphere.

The tournament itself is remembered as one in which the less experienced rugby playing nations, who – unlike four years previously – had to qualify to participate, stood up to be counted against senior opponents. The tournament also grew commercially, for both the IRFB and host nations, generating almost 10 times the revenue of the 1987 competition.

On the pitch, Pool A began with reigning champions New Zealand going head-to-head with England at Twickenham, the All Blacks winning 18-12, with flanker Michael Jones scoring the only try. It was no surprise that the All Blacks went on to finish top of the pool and England finish runners-up, with both teams beating Italy and the USA, although the All Blacks were tested in their clash with the Azzurri before coming through 31-21 winners.

Scotland and Ireland were the teams to take the top two places in Pool B, as expected, with the Scots finishing in prime position following their 25-15 success over the Irish. In this group, at least, the minnows of Japan and Zimbabwe never threatened to cause an upset.

This was not the case in Pool C, where Wales suffered a shock 9-3 defeat to debutants Western Samoa at Cardiff Arms Park, effectively ending their hopes of reaching the last eight – the minimum requirement for a team which four years ago had won the bronze medal. Samoa followed up this success with a 35-12 victory over Argentina to reach the knockout stages, while eventual champions Australia won all of their matches to top the pool.

Pool D, which was comfortably won by France, also witnessed an unexpected result when Canada overcame Fiji, the darlings of the 1987 competition, to claim the runners-up spot. The 13-3 success over the Fijians in Bayonne was built on the accurate goal kicking of Gareth Rees, after which the confident Canucks then defeated Romania 19-11.

The quarter-finals began with England beating France 19-10 in Paris in a tough match which will be remembered for a no-nonsense, momentum-shifting tackle by Mickey Skinner on Marc Cecillion. Tries by winger Rory Underwood and Captain Will Carling delivered England a semi-final contest against Scotland, who had ended the dreams of Western Samoa with a 28-6 victory. In what came to be known as the clash of the tournament, Australia fought back from behind to edge past Ireland 19-18 at Lansdowne Park, thanks to a dramatic late try from fly-half Michal Lynagh. They would then go on to face New Zealand in the second semi-final, after the holders had dispatched a plucky Canada team 29-13.

The Wallabies went on to win the Southern Hemisphere semi against the All Blacks 16-6 with David Campese and Tom Horan bagging crucial tries. It was a momentous triumph for the Aussies and a first ever Rugby World Cup defeat for New Zealand.

The other semi – between Northern Hemisphere rivals England and Scotland at Murrayfield – was determined by Rob Andrew's drop-goal, which earned England a tense 9-6 victory.

After New Zealand had finished third by beating Scotland 19-6 in the bronze medal match, Australia were crowned world champions after producing some flowing rugby to beat England

12-6, despite the hosts attempting to play a more open style. Tom Horan scored the only try of the match in front of a crowd of 56,203 at Twickenham.

Tournament stats:

Teams: 16

Matches: 32

Total Attendance: 1,060,065

Leading points scorers: 68 – Ralph Keyes (Ire); 66 – Michael Lynagh (Aus); 61 – Gavin Hastings (Sco); 56 – Jonathan Webb (Eng); 44 – Grant Fox (NZ).

Leading try scorers: 6 – David Campese (Aus), Jean-Baptiste Lafond (Fra); 4 – Tim Horan (Aus), Brian Robinson (Ire), Iwan Tukalo (Sco), Rory Underwood (Eng).

Gate receipts: £23.3 million

Global television audience: 1.75 billion

SOUTH AFRICA HOSTS THE 1995 RUGBY WORLD CUP

While the backdrop to the 1995 tournament was one of increasing demands in order for the game to become professional, and elite players once again signing up for a potential rebel event, the memory will always be that of a colourful tournament won by hosts South Africa in their first World Cup after being readmitted to the sporting fold since the dismantling of the Apartheid regime. The image of President Nelson Mandela handing the Webb Ellis Cup to Springboks' captain Francois Pienaar captured the spirit of the new Rainbow Nation, ultimately heralding a change of direction for rugby itself. Both South Africa and the sport were at a crossroads in their histories. An emotional tournament deserved a fitting final, and although the rugby on show was not attractive, the contest was tense, as the Springboks memorably beat New Zealand 15-12 after extra-time.

South Africa began the tournament on the front foot by overcoming holders Australia 27-18 in the opening match, going on to win Pool A following successes over Romania (21-8) and Canada (20-0). The Wallabies had the consolation of finishing second in the pool.

England and Western Samoa claimed the top two spots in Pool B, with the crucial clash between them going to England 44-22 as Rory Underwood scored two tries and Neil Back one, while they were also awarded a penalty try. Italy and Argentina were the two teams from the pool to miss out on reaching the knockout stages.

Pool C was the most entertaining as New Zealand initially muscled their way past Ireland 43-19 before going on to a record-breaking 145-17 victory over Japan. The All Blacks scored 21 tries, six of which came from winger Marc Ellis. In what looked like a tough pool on paper, the All Blacks finished off with a 34-9 success over Wales. The pool ended with a scrap for second place, which was won by Ireland who narrowly overcame rivals Wales 24-23 in Johannesburg. Eddie Halvey, Nick Popplewell and Denis McBride were the try-scorers for the Irish.

After France and Scotland had both easily beaten Tonga and debutants Ivory Coast, the top two places in Pool D were decided by the head-to-head between the two Northern Hemisphere adversaries. It was a tactical affair which Les Bleus eventually won 22-19 in order to claim the top spot.

The low point of the tournament was also seen earlier in this pool when Ivory Coast winger Max Brito was left paralysed from the neck down after being crushed under a pile of players in the 29-11 defeat to Tonga.

The first of the quarter-finals was won by France who got the better of Ireland 36-12 in a match which saw Thierry Lacoste kick a record eight penalties. In keeping with what was to become a high-scoring round, South Africa were too powerful for Western Samoa, winning 42-14 with winger Chester Williams taking the headlines with four tries. The plum tie of the round was England against cup holders Australia at Newlands in Cape Town, a nervy contest which England edged 25-22 thanks to a successful last-minute drop-goal from Rob Andrew. In a last quarter-final clash which produced nine tries – six of which went to the All Blacks – Scotland were beaten 48-30 to set up two very different semi-finals.

In swamp-like conditions at King's Park in Durban, Ruben Kruger scored the only try of the match as South Africa reached the final by narrowly beating France 19-15. The second semi in Cape Town will be remembered as the day All Blacks winger Jonah Lomu left an impression on world rugby and on England's tentative defence, especially winger Tony Underwood. England were unable to shackle the 20-year-old and future world star of the game, who bulldozed his way to four tries in the 45-29 victory – a brace of tries each for Rory Underwood and Will Carling counting for little. England completed their tournament by losing the bronze medal match to France 19-9, with Olivier Roumat and Emile Ntamack scoring the only tries.

The final was a slightly tedious, if engrossing, kicking game which ended 12-12 after 80 minutes with Joel Stransky slotting three penalties and a drop-goal for the Springboks, and Andrew Mehrtens kicking all the All Blacks' points and almost winning it for his side with a late drop-goal attempt. The match was decided in extra-time when Stransky nailed a drop-goal between the posts to earn the Springboks an emotional and historic victory.

Once again the Rugby World Cup had captured the imagination of a worldwide audience, but this one also brought down the curtain on the sport being completely amateur at all levels. Two months after Francois Pienaar lifted the Webb Ellis Cup, the IRFB allowed rugby to go professional.

Tournament stats:

Teams: 16

Matches: 32

Total Attendance: 938,436

Leading points scorers: 112 - Thiery Lacroix (Fra); 104 – Gavin Hastings (Sco); 84 – Andrew Mehrtens (NZ); 79 – Rob Andrew (Eng); 61 – Joel Stransky (SA).

Leading try scorers: 7 – Marc Ellis (NZ), Jonah Lomu (NZ); 5 – Gavin Hastings (Sco), Rory Underwood (Eng); 4 – Thierry Lacroix (Fra), Adriaan Richter (SA), Chester Williams (SA).

Gate receipts: £30.3 million

Global television audience: 2.67 billion

WALES HOSTS THE 1999 RUGBY WORLD CUP

Wales officially hosted the 1999 Rugby World Cup which, for the first time, had expanded into a 20-team tournament divided into five pools of four. The pool winners would automatically go through to the quarter-finals, while the five pool runners-up and the best third-placed team would compete in a quarter-final play-off, from which the three winners would also progress to the last eight.

The Principality hosted nine of the 41 matches with the remainder taking place in England (nine), Scotland (eight), France (eight) and Ireland (seven). It was also the first World Cup of the professional era, but some things remained unchanged as the Southern Hemisphere teams continued to dominate the tournament, and Australia were deservedly crowned champions for the second time.

Wales opened the proceedings with a narrow 23-18 victory over Argentina in the newly-built Millennium Stadium in Cardiff, a result which helped them finish top of Pool D on points difference, but not before they suffered a surprise 38-31 defeat to

Samoa. Runners-up Samoa and third-placed Argentina, who also both finished on seven points, reached the quarter-final play-offs.

Pool A was won by undefeated South Africa with Scotland in second place. The clash between debutants Uruguay and Spain, who had both reached the finals through the new qualifying repechage system, was won by the South Americans to ensure they finished third.

Pool B offered up no surprises as New Zealand overcame Tonga, Italy and England – beating the latter 30-16 at Twickenham. England finished runners-up.

Pool C also witnessed the senior teams take charge with France taking top spot and Fiji claiming second place ahead of Canada and Namibia.

In the final group, Pool E, Australia shone with successes over Ireland – who were to finish as runners-up – Romania and USA.

The new, mid-week quarter-final play-off system now came into effect, producing one unexpected result when Argentina edged past Ireland 28-24 in Lens, France with Diego Luis Albanese scoring the only try. The other play-off matches saw the Clive Woodward-coached England team beat Fiji 45-24, and Scotland ease away from Samoa 35-20 at Murrayfield.

The most memorable of the subsequent quarter-finals was South Africa's 44-21 victory over England during which Springboks fly-half Jannie de Beer successfully converted five drop-goals, a World Cup record, on his way to a personal points tally of 34. South Africa's win put them in the semi-finals where they were to meet an Australia team who ended the cup hopes of hosts Wales when they won 24-9 in Cardiff. No.9 George Gregan starred with two tries for the Wallabies. Elsewhere in the quarter-finals, the All Blacks were too powerful for Scotland in their 30-18 win, while France put down a plucky Argentina side 47-25.

The semi-final stage produced two memorable clashes – perhaps the matches of the tournament – as Australia met South Africa, and France faced New Zealand, both at Twickenham. The Wallabies eventually edged past the Springboks 27-21 in a match which needed extra-time to divide these two equally matched teams. In a contest which bore no tries, it was the kicking of Jannie de Beer (who slotted six penalties and drop-goal for South Africa) and Matthew Burke (who added to his tally for Australia with eight penalties) which dominated. Stephan Larkham dropped a goal in extra-time to confirm the Wallabies' passage into the final.

In a remarkable second semi, France came back from 31-9 down to stun a New Zealand side which had been in total control after two tries from Jonah Lomu. Les Bleus scored 33 unanswered points to win 41-31, their four tries being shared by Christophe Lamaison, Christophe Dominici, Richard Dourthe and Phillipe Bernat-Salles. The All Blacks were to lose again before the tournament ended, as they went down 22-18 to South Africa in the bronze medal match.

France, after their triumph over the All Blacks, were unable to raise their game one more time for the final losing 35-12 to an Australian side propelled to victory by Matthew Burke who scored 25 points. In front of more than 72,000 at the Millennium Stadium, Aussie skipper John Eales lifted the Webb Ellis Cup which was presented to him by Her Majesty Queen Elizabeth II.

Tournament stats:

Teams: 20

Matches: 41

Total Attendance: 1,562,427

Leading points scorers: 102 – Gonzalo Quesada (Arg); 101 - Matt Burke (Aus); 97 – Jannie de Beer (SA); 79 – Andrew Mehrtens (NZ); 69 – Jonny Wilkinson (Eng).

Leading try scorers: 8 – Jonah Lomu (NZ), Jeff Wilson (NZ); 4 – Keith Wood (Ire), Phillipe Bernay-Salles (Fra), Viliame Satala (Fij), Dan Luger (Eng).

Gate receipts: £70 million

Global television audience: 3.10 billion

AUSTRALIA HOSTS THE 2003 RUGBY WORLD CUP

England, under the guidance of perfectionist head coach Clive Woodward and feisty captain Martin Johnson, took their strongest, most in-form and best funded squad ever to a World Cup, duly delivering on their potential by lifting the Webb Ellis Cup. However, this first World Cup victory for a Northern Hemisphere team did not come easy for the favourites who stuttered before beating hosts Australia 20-17 in the final, thanks to a memorable drop-goal in extra-time by player of the tournament Jonny Wilkinson.

The competition was supposed to be co-hosted by Australia and New Zealand, but contractual disputes over signage rights at New Zealand grounds meant Australia staged the 20-team event using 10 venues around the country. The tournament was again refigured, this time into four pools of five teams, with the top two going automatically into the quarter-finals.

The first of the 48 matches to be played in the 42-day tournament saw the Wallabies dispatch Argentina 24-8 en route to winning Pool A, after thrashing Namibia (by a record-breaking 142-0), Romania (90-8) and then squeezing past biggest threat Ireland (17-16).

Pool B also went with seniority as France and Scotland, in that order, claimed the top two places. However, while Les Bleus eased through all of their matches, the Scots suffered a humbling 51-9 setback to France which they followed up with a crucial 22-20 win over Fiji thanks largely to Chris Paterson who kicked 17 points.

In Pool C, Samoa, Uruguay and Georgia played second fiddle to heavyweights England and South Africa whose showdown at Perth was won by England 25-6; Will Greenwood scored the only try to which was added 20 points from the boot of Wilkinson.

This ensured top spot for Woodward's men although they did have a scare earlier in the pool when they were cited for briefly having 16 players on the pitch in the unconvincing 35-22 victory over Samoa. They were given a warning but were not docked points.

New Zealand blitzed their way through Pool D beating Italy 70-7, Canada 68-6, and Tonga 91-7. They finished top of the pool after beating Wales 53-37 in Sydney in a match which delivered 12 tries, eight of which were scored by the All Blacks.

The most nail-biting of the quarter-final clashes saw England beat Wales 28-17 in Brisbane, but not before Stephen Jones and Colin Jarvis had scored tries to give the Welsh a half-time advantage. Martyn Williams also added a third try for Wales, but it was not enough to overcome England who again leant heavily on the kicking of Wilkinson (23 points) building on a solitary Greenwood try.

New Zealand maintained their impressive momentum with a comfortable 29-9 dismantling of South Africa, as centre Leon MacDonald scored 16 points including one of his team's three tries. The two other last-eight ties went with form as Australia beat Scotland 33-16, with Elton Flatley bagging 18 points, while Frederick Michalak provided 23 points in France's 43-21 success over Ireland.

In pursuit of being the only team to retain the Webb Ellis Cup, Australia had to swerve New Zealand in the first semi in Sydney in front of more than 82,000 spectators and, against the odds, found some eye-catching rhythm in winning 22-10. Flatley again came to the fore kicking five penalties as Stirling Mortlock dotted down for the Wallabies.

In the all-Northern Hemisphere semi, talisman Wilkinson again proved nerveless in kicking all the points for England with five penalties and three drop-goals, as they beat France 24-7. New

Zealand finished the tournament in third place after winning the bronze medal match against France 40-13, scoring six tries.

Almost 83,000 excited fans were in the Telstra Stadium, Sydney for the final between old sporting adversaries Australia and England. They were about to witness a classic.

Winger Lote Tuqiri gave the Wallabies an early lead but, in a tight contest, his opposite number for England, Jason Robinson, also scored a try. Flatley and Wilkinson recorded four penalties each to take the final into extra-time. In this gripping match, controlled by the two kickers, it was Wilkinson who memorably came out on top when his slightly scuffed, right-foot drop-goal on 100 minutes proved to be the difference between the teams.

It earned England and the Northern Hemisphere a first – and currently only – World Cup final triumph, and made coaching maestro Woodward, inspirational skipper Johnson and tournament top-scorer Wilkinson icons of the game in England.

Tournament stats:

Teams: 20

Matches: 48

Total Attendance: 1,837,547

Leading points scorers: 113 – Jonny Wilkinson (Eng); 103 – Frederic Michalak (Fra); 100 – Elton Flatley (Aus); 75 – Leon MacDonald (NZ); 71 – Chris Paterson (Sco).

Leading try scorers: 7 – Doug Howlett (NZ), Mils Muliaina (NZ); 6 – Joe Rokocoko (NZ), 5 – Will Greenwood (Eng), Chris Latham (Aus), Josh Lewsey Mat Rogers (Aus), Lote Tuqiri (Aus).

Gate receipts: £81.8 million

Global television audience: 3.40 billion

FRANCE HOSTS THE 2007 RUGBY WORLD CUP

This World Cup is remembered as one full of shock results, where England delivered an unexpectedly brave defence of their crown, the hosts failed to live up to expectations, and South Africa lifted the Webb Ellis Cup for a second time.

France won the bid to host the finals, despite competition from England, using the same venues as those for the 1998 FIFA World Cup. This ensured a greater number of seats being available to the paying public as compared to the 2003 tournament, with the smallest ground being the 33,900-seat Stade de la Mosson in Montpellier.

Sticking to the now familiar format of four pools of five teams – with 42 matches in France, four in Cardiff (Wales) and two in Edinburgh (Scotland) – this, the sixth Rugby World Cup, opened with a shattering 17-12 defeat for France at the hands of Argentina. It was the first time France had lost in the pool stages of a World Cup, and despite fighting back with wins over Georgia (64-7), Namibia (87-10) and, crucially, Ireland (25-3), Les Bleus finished runners-up to Argentina in Pool D. The unbeaten Pumas topped the pool, while Ireland (who narrowly beat minnows Georgia 14-10) could only finish third.

South Africa won Pool A after edging past Tonga 30-25 and trouncing USA 64-15 before a showdown with a faltering England – now coached by Brian Ashton – who they convincingly beat 36-0. The final between these two teams a few weeks later was to be a more even contest.

Wales was the most notable scalp taken in Pool B, failing to reach the quarter-finals after losing to pool winners Australia (32-20) and, more surprisingly, Fiji (38-34). Japan and Canada made up the numbers.

Pool C witnessed a typically ruthless performance from New Zealand who won all four of their matches, scoring 309 points and conceding just 35.

The first of the quarters was a rehash of the final four years before, and this too was a tense affair as England beat Australia 12-10 in Marseille with Jonny Wilkinson proving the difference with four penalties. The most unexpected result of the last eight saw France raise their game to another level to knock out Graham Henry's All Blacks, the 20-18 victory in Cardiff being secured after tries by Thierry Dusautoir and Yannick Jauzion.

Argentina's 19-13 success over Scotland was less of a surprise given the Pumas' form in the tournament and the strength of their squad, put together by head coach Marcelo Loffreda, which included world class players like Agustin Pichot at scrum-half and centre Felipe Contepomi.

The last quarter-final tie witnessed South Africa maintain their momentum in scoring five tries in the 37-20 victory over Fiji.

In front of more than 80,000 in the Stade de France in Paris, England put their patchy form behind them to overcome hosts France 14-9 in the first semi-final, with winger Josh Lewsey dramatically scoring the only try of the match after two minutes. The second semi went to form as South Africa ended the impressive tournament of Argentina, winning 37-13 as wing sensation Bryan Habana grabbed two of the Springboks' four tries. The bronze medal match is often the one which no team wants to play because it acts as a reminder of how close they came to reaching the final.

But this was not the case for Argentina who were enjoying the most successful World Cup in their history. This showed as they scored five tries – three coming from Contepomi – in the 34-10 victory over a forlorn France side.

The final followed the pattern of many before, a slightly nervous affair where running rugby played second fiddle to the kicking game. And it was in this respect that South Africa came out on top against holders England, winning 15-6 as Percy Montgomery struck four penalties and Francois Steyn one. Wilkinson slotted two penalties for England who came closest to a try when winger Mark Cueto touched down only for the effort to be ruled out because of a foot in touch.

Tournament stats:

Teams: 20

Matches: 48

Total Attendance: 2,263,223

Leading points scorers: 105 - Percy Montgomery (SA); 91 – Felipe Contepomi (Arg); 67 – Jonny Wilkinson (Eng); 50 – Nick Evans (NZ); 47 – Jean-Baptiste Elissalde (Aus).

Leading try scorers: 8 – Bryan Habana (SA); 7 – Drew Mitchell (NZ); 6 – Doug Howlett (NZ), Shane Williams (Wal); 5 – Joe Rokocoko (NZ), Vincent Clerc (Fra), Chris Latham (Aus).

Gate receipts: £147 million

Global television audience: 4 billion

NEW ZEALAND HOSTS THE 2011 RUGBY WORLD CUP

The All Blacks had been the powerhouse of rugby for more than 20 years, starting most World Cups as favourites, yet only winning once in 1987. Despite concerns over the number of visitors, especially those making the long trip from Europe, and the initial lack of interest from potential sponsors and commercial partners, rugby's world governing body, the IRB, named New Zealand as the 2011 Rugby World Cup hosts. It was a chance for Aotearoa (the Land of the Long White Cloud) to propel itself onto the world's sporting stage, one which it took with both hands.

Commercially, the tournament was more of a success than many believed it could be and, on the pitch, the All Blacks capped off the largest sporting event ever held in their country by winning a nail-biting final against France. The 20 teams involved were the same as four years before, apart from Russia who qualified in place of Portugal.

The competition began perfectly for the eventual champions – led by inspirational captain Richie McCaw – as they beat Tonga 41-10 en route to remaining unbeaten in winning Pool A. The All Blacks also overcame France 37-17 in the pool, meaning the Northern Hemisphere side were to finish second in the pool, but were more prepared for when the two teams met again in the final. However, France were far from convincing against Canada and Japan, and surprisingly lost 19-14 to a competitive Tonga team.

In Pool B, England finished top and unbeaten, but only by virtue of narrow wins over runners-up Argentina (13-9) and third-placed Scotland (16-12). Although not at his metronomic best, Jonny Wilkinson was again at the sharp end for England, the fly-half crucially kicking 17 points in these two low scoring contests.

Pool C put Ireland and Australia on a collision course; a match-up which has produced some classic encounters over the years. This one was to be equally tight with the Irish beating the Wallabies 15-6 to top the pool leaving the losers to take second place.

The top two places in Pool D were fought over by South Africa and Wales, the former winning the crucial head-to-head 17-16 thanks to tries from Francois Steyn and Francois Hougaard. Both teams had few problems getting past Samoa, Fiji and Namibia in the other pool matches. New Zealand faced Argentina in the quarter-finals but did so without influential fly-half Dan Carter, who had earlier suffered an injured groin ending his tournament.

The All Blacks, now with Colin Slade at stand-off, hit their straps in beating Argentina 33-10, sending them through to a semi-final against Australia who scraped through following a tense 11-9 success over holders South Africa with the winning points coming from the boot of James O'Connor.

Wales beat Ireland 22-10 to reach the last four where they would face a France side buoyed by their 19-12 victory over England in a match they always controlled.

This was not the case in their semi-final against Wales in Auckland. However, three penalties were enough to earn Les Bleus a 9-8 win against a Welsh side which scored the only try through Mike Phillips and had captain Sam Warburton dismissed after 20 minutes.

New Zealand laid down a marker for the final with a stunning performance to ease past Australia 20-6 in the second semi-final – Ma'a Nonu scoring the only try of the game. Australia won the bronze medal match beating Wales 21-18, despite the Welshmen scoring a last-minute try from Leigh Halfpenny.

The final, in front of more than 61,000 at Eden Park in Auckland, was a close call as New Zealand failed to find their trademark fluency while France proved they were up for the fight. The All Blacks took the lead when Tony Woodcock dotted down after 15 minutes, to which was added a second half penalty from Stephen Donald. The 8-0 advantage lasted just one minute before Thierry Dusautoir scored a try, converted by Francois Trinh-Duc, on 47 minutes to make the score 8-7. France seemed the most likely to score next, and went close with a Trinh-Duc penalty, but the All Blacks kept them at bay to record a second Rugby World Cup triumph almost a quarter of a century after their first.

Tournament stats:

Teams: 20

Matches: 48

Total Attendance: 1,477,294

Leading points scorers: 62 – Morne Steyne (SA), 52 – James O'Connor (Aus); 46 – Kurt Morath (Ton); 44 - Ronan O'Gara (Ire); 41 – Piri Weepu (NZ).

Leading try scorers: 6 – Chris Ashton (Eng), Vincent Clerc (Fra); 5 – Adam Ashley-Cooper (Aus), Keith Ellis (Ire), Israel Dagg (NZ); 4 – Mark Cueto (Eng), Vereniki Goneva (Fij), Richard Kahui (NZ).

Gate receipts: £131 million

Global television audience: 4 billion

ENGLAND HOSTS THE 2015 RUGBY WORLD CUP

England out-bid rivals Italy, Japan and South Africa to win the right to host this World Cup, bringing the tournament back to the birthplace of rugby for the first time since 1999. The bid was won on the back of the quality of the stadia available, the projected growth in interest in the sport and, probably most importantly, the revenues which would be generated for the game.

The governing body World Rugby, which changed its name from the IRB in 2014, was projected to earn around £300 million from this eighth World Cup, with around £220 million coming from commercial gains and £80 million from the fee paid by the host nation. The tournament eventually eclipsed all commercial expectations, seeing almost 2.50 million tickets sold, extending the reach of the tournament to new markets, particularly in Europe.

On the pitch, it was New Zealand who broke the records, being the first team to both retain the Webb Ellis Cup and lift it for a third time, after beating Australia 34-17 in the final at Twickenham. The Southern Hemisphere teams continued to dominate the sport's showpiece as South Africa overcame Argentina 24-13 to take the bronze medal. For the first time, no Northern Hemisphere team reached the semi-finals, particularly disappointing for a tournament being held in Europe.

As was now the norm, 20 teams were divided into four pools of five with Pool A becoming known as the 'pool of death,' as it featured Australia, England, Wales, Fiji and minnows Uruguay. The group lived up to its billing as hosts England exited the cup at this stage, after shallow and toothless performances in losing 28-25 to Wales and 33-13 to Australia. Head coach Stuart Lancaster, who had previously been given a contract extension to 2020, departed his role soon after.

The Aussies and the Welsh proceeded into the quarter-finals, as did South Africa and Scotland from Pool B, but not before what is considered the most memorable upset in World Cup history. The first game of the pool witnessed Japan, coached by Eddie Jones, beat South Africa 34-32 in Brighton, coming from behind to score the last of their three tries in the final minute through Karne Hesketh. Full-back Ayumu Goromaru scored a try and kicked 19 points in what was to be Japan's greatest ever World Cup result and the Springboks' lowest ebb. Japan, nicknamed the Brave Blossoms, narrowly failed to reach the knockout stages following a 45-10 defeat to Scotland.

New Zealand won the crucial Pool C clash with Argentina 26-16, meaning they finished in top spot, while the Pumas were second, both being far too strong for Georgia, Tonga and Namibia.

Pool D also failed to throw up any surprises as Ireland and France shone, with the Irish taking first place after beating Les Bleus 24-9 in the final match of the pool at the Millennium Stadium, one of eight matches to be played at the Cardiff-based ground.

The quarter-finals, which featured four Northern Hemisphere teams against four from the Southern Hemisphere, began with South Africa fortunate to edge past Wales 23-19. Wales had been the better team for most of the contest, but the Springboks came through after a 75th minute try from scrum-half Fourie du Preez.

This set up a semi-final against New Zealand who reached this stage after scoring nine tries – three from powerful winger Julian Savea – in the 62-13 thumping of France. The third quarter-final saw Argentina upset the odds by taking a 20-3 advantage over Ireland, before beating them 43-20 and scoring four tries while world class fly-half Nicolas Sanchez notched 25 points with a faultless kicking performance.

The last quarter-final delivered the keenest fought match of the competition with Australia holding off a Scotland fightback to win 35-34. A late, disputed penalty was slotted by Bernard Foley to earn the Wallabies victory. Match referee Craig Joubert was widely criticised for the penalty decision, extraordinarily even by World Rugby in a public statement after the match.

In the first semi, New Zealand had to work hard to break down a stubborn South Africa side who led 12-7 at half-time. The All Blacks got the job done by scoring the only two tries of the match, the crucial second coming from Beauden Barrett.

Adam Ashley-Cooper scored three of Australia's four tries in their comfortable 29-15 win over Argentina in the second semi. Argentina, who had enjoyed an impressive tournament, were worn down by South Africa in the third-place final at London's Olympic Stadium with the 24-13 score-line being a fair reflection of the match.

In the first ever Australia versus New Zealand Rugby World Cup final, a largely dominant All Blacks extended their half-time lead of 16-3 to win 34-17 come the final whistle. They scored three tries and Dan Carter, who limped out of the competition four years earlier with an injury, kicked 19 points.

Tournament stats:

Teams: 20

Matches: 48

Total Attendance: 2,477,805

Leading points scorers: 97 – Nicolas Sanchez (Arg); 93 - Handre Pollard (SA); 82 – Bernard Foley (Aus); 82 – Dan Carter (NZ); 79 – Greg Laidlaw (Sco).

Leading try scorers: 8 – Julian Savea (NZ); 6 – Nehe Milner-Skudder (NZ); 5 – Bryan Habana (SA), Gareth Davies (Wal), Juan Imhoff (Arg), JP Pietersen (SA).

Gate receipts: £160 million

Global television audience: 4.25 billion

SIX OF THE BEST RUGBY WORLD CUP MEMORIES

1987: FIJI THE BRAVE

The build-up to a major tournament can be a time of mixed emotions for players, coaches, officials and fans. The fitness of key players is scrutinised, there is speculation whether the team can maintain recent momentum or cast aside indifferent form, and there is nervous tension about the battles ahead. The list of potential concerns, even for a committed optimistic, is always present until the contest begins in earnest. However, these are trivial in comparison to what the Fiji team faced ahead of the inaugural World Cup starting in New Zealand in 1987.

The squad, coached by Kiwi George Simpkin, had moved to an army base to complete its preparations for the World Cup amid much excitement in the country. Fiji is a nation comprised of some 300 islands with rugby as one of its unifying forces. Almost 10 percent of the population are registered players. The excitement in the country was soon dampened when, eight days before the start of the inaugural World Cup, a military coup led by Lieutenant Colonel Sitiveri Rabuka took control of the country.

All communications with, and flights to, the outside world were ended, threatening to prevent Fiji from taking part in the tournament. The World Cup organisers were so concerned that they were on the verge of officially asking Western Samoa, who were secretly on standby as first reserve, to replace Fiji. This never occurred because, despite the political uncertainty, the team were allowed to leave the country and take their place at the tournament.

This was not the end of the Fiji story who, under such taxing circumstances, made their mark on the competition, winning the hearts of the worldwide sporting community by playing an exciting brand of rugby which took them to the quarter-finals.

Fiji began the tournament by scoring four tries in beating Argentina 28-9. They then rested players for the clash with New Zealand, which was lost 74-13, ahead of the crucial contest against Scotland. Fiji narrowly lost 18-15 to the Scots, leaving both teams, plus Argentina, level on two points. Fiji claimed the runners-up spot and a place in the last eight by scoring more tries than their rivals. This set up an entertaining quarter-final with France against whom Fiji maintained their entertaining, high risk approach to the game. Fly-half Severo Koroduadua and centres Tomasi Cama and Kaiava Salusalu were at the forefront of the Fijians' efforts, before Les Bleus eventually capitalised on numerous errors to win 31-16.

This was the end of the World Cup journey for Fiji, but they departed as every neutral fan's favourite team, having chiselled out an exciting template for future Fijian teams to follow.

1999: LES BLEUS TAME THE ALL BLACKS

France's memorable comeback to thump cup favourites New Zealand 45-31 in the 1999 semi-final was a fillip – albeit temporarily – for French rugby, the game in the Northern Hemisphere and those who like their rugby silky and smooth rather than powerful and strong.

With the irresistible Jonah Lomu on the wing, the All Blacks had been rampant, coming into the contest against France having scored 205 points and conceding just 46, in matches against England, Tonga, Italy and Scotland. Les Bleus were also unbeaten, having overcome Fiji, Canada, Namibia and Argentina. However, they had been far less convincing, which turned out to be the case in the initial period of the semi-final held at Twickenham in London.

Lomu, who was to finish the World Cup as leading try scorer with eight, scored two typically bull-like tries as the All Blacks led 24-10 in what had been a dominant first half. They were expected to continue in that manner in the second period, thus setting up a final against Australia. The match, in front of a crowd of 70,000, was then turned on its head, and the tournament likewise, when France fought back in a style which few teams can replicate. Two drop goals and two penalties from fly-half Christophe Lamaison sent them on their way before Christophe Dominici ran in a spectacular try, and victory was sealed with a late score from Phillipe Bernat-Sailes. France had come from behind against the best team in the world by playing with Gallic fair and considerable pride.

The All Blacks had few answers to their opponents' unpredictability, falling back on their go-to plan of giving the ball to Lomu and hoping he could smash through the French defence, but when that failed, so did they. Unfortunately for France, they were unable to reach these heights one more time in the final against Australia which they lost 35-12. It left them then, as they are now, probably the best team in the world never to have lifted the Webb Ellis Cup; that famous unpredictability being both their greatest strength and Achilles heel.

1995: THE BOKS ARE BACK

It is perhaps the most iconic image in Rugby World Cup history, that moment when President Nelson Mandela presented South Africa captain Francois Pienaar with the Webb Ellis Cup after the host nation had narrowly beaten New Zealand 15-12 in the final after extra-time.

Both men were leaders, both top of their chosen fields, and both, of course, wearing a green Springboks jersey with the No.6 embossed in gold on the back. This emotional moment between these two inspirational men was beamed into billions of television sets and printed on the front and back pages of countless newspapers around the world. Such was its impact globally that it even inspired a best-selling book on which the Hollywood movie Invictus, directed by Clint Eastwood, was based.

Politically, it showed the world that South Africa was making steps towards becoming the 'rainbow nation' and leaving the scourge of the Apartheid behind. It offered hope that this divided country was beginning to unify, and that rugby – always considered a white man's game – could become one of its building blocks.

From a sporting perspective, the Springboks had just hosted and won the first Rugby World Cup that they had been allowed to enter after the fall of Apartheid. It was no mean feat, and one not lost on a sports-mad country which had been given little to cheer about for many years.

After being presented with the Webb Ellis Cup on that historic day at Ellis Park, Johannesburg, in front of almost 60,000 spectators, Pienaar later said that he had wanted to hug Mandela but did not because it 'was not appropriate'. He added: "Mandela said 'thank you very much for what you've done for South Africa', but I said, 'thank you for what you have done'. Then I lifted the trophy which was unbelievable. I can't describe the feeling as it wouldn't do it justice."

The match itself had been memorable too despite failing to produce a try, as a well-honed South African defence blunted New Zealand's attacking prowess. The match was finally won in extra-time through Joel Stransky's drop goal. It was the type of climax to a tournament which would normally be the defining moment. But that came a few minutes later when two proud Africans met for a few seconds and, with smiles on their faces, exchanged the Webb Ellis Cup, both knowing that nothing in their worlds would ever be the same again.

2003: WILKINSON DELIVERS FOR ENGLAND

England were favourites to win the Rugby World Cup in Australia in 2003, which they did, but it could not have been tighter or more dramatic.

The final in Sydney delivered the first and only victory for a Northern Hemisphere team, vindicating the professional coaching ethos of Clive Woodward and confirming fly-half Jonny Wilkinson as a worldwide rugby superstar. England had been the best team in the world for the previous two seasons and their game plan was simple; defend like demons, be powerful up front and allow Wilkinson to kick them to glory.

This got them to the final against hosts Australia, but despite a controlled performance they could not shake off the Wallabies who had their own kicking sensation on the day. The match went into extra-time after Wilkinson collected three penalties to add to Jason Robinson's try. However, Australia's Elton Flatley also held his nerve to kick three penalties which, in addition to Lote Tuqiri's early try, meant extra-time. Both players also scored a penalty apiece in extra-time, leaving the score at 17-17 and both teams facing the prospect of sudden death for the first time in a World Cup.

This tense, nerve-wracking contest was finally decided in the last of the 100 minutes played when the left-footed Wilkinson hesitantly struck a drop goal with his right foot, which crept between the posts and over the bar.

Nothing captures this moment in rugby history better than the iconic commentary from BBC radio's Ian Robertson, delivered in that rasping Scottish brogue which, with the drama unfolding, had been pushed to breaking point. "Martin Johnson has it," he said. "There's 35 seconds to go. This is the one. It's coming back for Jonny Wilkinson. He drops for World Cup glory. It's up. It's over! He's done it. Jonny Wilkinson is England's hero again." He added: "And there's no time for Australia to come back. England have just won the World Cup." It proved to be the pinnacle for both England and Wilkinson.

It was no surprise that many of the England team – which had been dubbed Dad's Army ahead of the tournament – retired after the victory, and while Wilkinson would compete in two more World Cups, injuries and insecurities took their toll on his performances. However, regardless of what was to follow, Wilkinson, with that tournament-winning drop goal, will always be remembered as the arch-finisher of a world-beating team and the man who restored sporting pride to a nation.

1991: AUSTRALIA SNATCH VICTORY FROM IRELAND'S GRASP

Matches between Australia and Ireland have often been hard fought and close; the very first in 1927 ended 5-3 to the Wallabies, setting the template for the next 91 years. None were closer than on October 20, 1991 at Lansdowne Road, Dublin in the quarter-finals of the Rugby World Cup – a match which will linger long in memory.

The Wallabies would go on to beat New Zealand 16-6 in the semis and hosts England 12-6 in the final, but not before a last-gasp 19-18 victory over a determined Ireland on home soil. The score was 15-12 to Australia with five minutes remaining when Irish flanker Gordon Hamilton scored a try which seemed to have decided the fate of the contest, certainly in the eyes of the partisan crowd, some of whom spilled over onto the pitch. But it was not over. Stand-in Aussie captain Michael Lynagh bravely called a backline move from a scrum, rather than going for a drop goal to level the score, and it was he who bagged the winning try in the final seconds after Jason Little and David Campese had made inroads.

Reflecting on the match later, Lynagh said: "It was the best moment of my career. It's something I am very proud of, to have steered the team in the right direction. For the team, it was a realisation that this was a pretty special group of people."

The 1991 head-to-head between these two proud rugby nations is one to remember, but it also started a timeline in which future matches would go to the wire.

Since then, Ireland have faced Australia three times in World Cups, losing 23-3 (1999) and 17-16 (2003), and winning 15-6 (2011), again most of the time there being little between the teams. In the last four years, it is Ireland who have held the upper hand, winning four of the last five clashes, all by a whisker (26-23, 27-24, 9-18, 26-21, 20-16).

2015: JAPAN DELIVERS GREATEST RUGBY WORLD CUP SHOCK

It was only the second time Japan had won a match at the Rugby World Cup, the first being against Zimbabwe in 1991. However, it set the tournament alight and emphasised the team's nickname – the Brave Blossoms.

The second day of the 2015 tournament in England began with Georgia surprisingly beating Tonga 17-10 in Pool C at Kingsholm in Gloucester. However, even this notable result was eclipsed a few hours later when rugby minnows Japan scored a late try to defeat two-time champions South Africa 34-32 at the Brighton Community Stadium. It was unquestionably the greatest shock in the 28-year history of the competition.

The Brave Blossoms, coached by the crafty Eddie Jones who had been part of the Springboks' coaching team when South Africa lifted the Webb Ellis Cup in 2007, stuck to a game plan of keeping the ball away from Springboks' huge forwards and dangerous wingers, while defending and counter-rucking with all of their might. And it worked. It seemed as if the Springboks had edged past their highly motivated opponents when they led by three points with under two minutes remaining.

Then Coenie Oosterhuizen was shown a yellow card and Japan awarded a penalty. A successful kick for the posts would have earned Japan three points and a more than honourable draw. However, talismanic captain Michael Leitch decided his team should gamble and go for the try against a South African team down to 14 players. They succeeded with replacement winger Karne Hesketh scoring in the corner to shock the Springboks and delight the rest of the rugby community.

Japan coach Eddie Jones said afterwards: "It's quite incredible. We thought we could compete but to beat South Africa is a fantastic achievement for the team and it's a great day for Japanese rugby. Japan can only play one way, we've got a little team, so we have to move the ball around and cause problems. Today is just the start. The target now is to make the quarter-finals and we have got Scotland in four days' time so we cannot rest on our laurels. If you are a child in Japan, you will watch this and will want to play rugby for Japan in the next World Cup."

The Brave Blossoms went on to win three of their four pool matches, only losing to Scotland, but it was not enough for them to reach the knockout stages. The Springboks bounced back to finish top of the pool and eventually took the bronze medal by beating Argentina 24-13.

Whether Japan's memorable victory over South Africa has had a lasting impact on the game in their country may be measured by how well they perform at this year's Rugby World Cup in front of their own supporters.

CHAPTER 2
WELCOME TO JAPAN

JAPAN FACTS AND FIGURES

Capital and largest city: Tokyo (population circa 14,000,000)

Ethnicity: 98.50% Japanese (Yamayo, Ainu and Ryukyuan peoples)

Religion: Shinto 52%, Buddhism 35%, Shinto sects 4%, Christianity 2.5%

Emperor: Akihito (since January 1989)

Prime Minister: Shinzo Abe

Total area: 145,936 sq mi/377,973 sq km (61st in world)

Population: 126, 440,000 (10th in world)

Number of islands: 6,852

GDP: $6 trillion (3rd in the world)

Currency: Yen

Time zone: GMT +9

Driving side: Left

Life expectancy: men 81 years, women 88 years (3rd in world)

Elderly: 21% of population is over 65 years old (1st in world)

JAPAN FUN FACTS

Japan has more than 3,000 McDonald's restaurants, the largest number in any country outside the USA. The Japanese eat more fish than any other people in the world, approximately 17 million tons per year. More than 5 billion servings of instant ramen noodles are consumed in Japan each year. Kobe beef is a worldwide famous delicacy, with these cows receiving daily massages, and in summer being fed saké and beer mash.

The Japanese have such a low birth rate that there are more adult diapers sold than baby diapers. They have more pets than children.

The world's shortest escalator is in the basement of More's department store in Kawasaki, it has only five steps and is 32.8 inches (83.3 cm) high. Shinjuku station, Tokyo's main train station, is the busiest in the world with more than two million users daily. In Japan, Kit Kat bars come in unusual flavours like grilled corn, Camembert cheese, Earl Grey tea, grape, and wasabi.

The Japanese avoid the number four (shi) because it sounds the same as the word for death; tall buildings do not have a fourth floor. The imperial family of Japan descends from an unbroken lineage of nearly 2,000 years, the oldest royal family in the world.

SIX POPULAR TOURIST ATTRACTIONS

MOUNT FUJI

Japan's most recognisable landmark is Mount Fuji which is also the country's highest mountain reaching 3,776 metres. It is tall enough to be seen from Tokyo which is more than 60 miles away.

IMPERIAL PALACE

The Imperial Palace, in Tokyo, is still in use by the royal family, but parts, including the stunning 17th-century parks hemmed in by walls and moats, are open to the public. The famous Nijubashi Bridge, also known as the double bridge on account of its watery reflection, is one of the highlights of a tour.

GINZA

The high-energy, neon-lit Tokyo shopping district of Ginza is popular with tourists. Alongside the multitude of shops and arcades, it is also home to the famous Kabuki-za Theatre and Shimbashi Enbujo Theatre.

HIROSHIMA PEACE MEMORIAL PARK

Hiroshima Heiwa Kinen Kōen (Hiroshima Peace Memorial Park) is located on the site where the first atomic bomb struck on August 6, 1945 and attracts more than a million visitors every year. The park contains monuments, memorials, and museums relating to the events of that historic day.

KYOTO

The city of Kyoto, where the Imperial Family reside, is Japan's most important and historically significant cultural centre, attracting more than 10 million visitors per year. Much of the architecture of the city avoided damage in World War II, meaning that some of the buildings are more than 1,000 years old.

JAPANESE ALPS

Chūbu-Sangaku is one of Japan's most beautiful national parks in which lies the Hida Mountains, also known as the Japanese Alps. The region attracts large numbers of walkers and climbers in summer and skiers in winter, while the park's hot springs are also a draw.

HISTORY OF JAPAN

The first human inhabitants of Japan have been traced back to prehistoric times, with the first written reference to Japan found in the Chinese Book of Han in the first century AD. Between the fourth century and the ninth century, a divided Japan was brought together under one government, nominally controlled by the Emperor whose descendants still reign over the country today. Over the centuries, the power of the Emperor declined and was surpassed by the military clans and their armies of samurai warriors.

The Tokugawa shogunate oversaw a prosperous and peaceful era (1600–1868), but also imposed a strict class system while severing contact with the outside world. After the fall of the shogunate, the new rulers transformed this feudal country into an empire.

Although democracy and modern culture developed in the early 20th century, the military was the real power and overruled Japan's civilian leaders in the 1920s and 1930s. This led to the invasion of Manchuria in 1931, the attack on Pearl Harbour in 1941, and ultimately the war with the Allies in World War II.

Japan unconditionally surrendered on August 15, 1945, following the atomic bombings of Hiroshima and Nagasaki. The Allies occupied Japan until 1952, after which the country steadily became an economic heavyweight based on the electronics and car industries. There have been periods of stagnation in the economy since the 1990s, a disruptive earthquake and tsunami in 2011 and a serious nuclear power disaster.

GEOGRAPHY

The Japanese archipelago is mountainous and stretches northeast to southwest 3,000 km off the east of the Asian continent. It is located where four tectonic plates meet, has approximately 40 active volcanoes, and experiences around 1,000 earthquakes a year.

Two thirds of the country's surface is covered by steep mountains which are prone to erosion from rivers and mudslides. The volcanic soil that washes along the coastal plains, making up around 13% of the land mass, is extremely fertile land.

The mainly temperate climate allows long growing seasons, although there is a wet season in most areas during the summer.

SPORT

Japan enjoys a wide variety of sports, many imported from the western world, playing a significant part of the country's culture.

Baseball is unquestionably the country's most popular sport with the Nippon League being Japan's largest professional sports competition in terms of television ratings and spectators. Such is its popularity that even some school matches and tournaments are televised.

Baseball was introduced to Japan in 1872 by Horace Wilson, a teacher from the USA, with the first team being set up six years later and the professional era beginning in the 1920s. The rules are essentially those of Major League Baseball in the USA, but there are some technical differences. The Nippon League uses a smaller baseball, strike zone and playing field. Five Nippon League teams have fields so small that they would break the official baseball rules in the USA. Japan has won the international World Baseball Classic twice, in 2006 and 2009.

However, Sumo wrestling is considered the country's national sport, with martial arts such as judo, karate and modern kendo being mostly popular on an amateur basis.

Football (soccer) in Japan is popular and the J-League has expanded rapidly in the last two decades, attracting players from around the world. The national team has reached every World Cup final since 1998, and in that year were ranked ninth in the world.

Tokyo will host the 2020 Olympics after beating Istanbul and Madrid in the bidding process, bringing the games back to Japan for the first time since 1964. Twenty-eight of the 33 venues in Tokyo are within five miles of the Olympic Village, and 11 new venues are being constructed. The Tokyo Games will feature karate, sport climbing, surfing and skateboarding for the first time, and the return of baseball and softball which were removed after 2008. Several disciplines in numerous core Olympic sports will also be added including freestyle BMX and the popular urban sport of three-a-side basketball which uses one hoop.

The overall cost of hosting the Olympics in Japan has risen dramatically since the bid was won and is now, according to the country's independent Board of Audit, on course to be $25 billion.

The most popular professional sports in Japan are:

1. Baseball
2. Soccer
3. Tennis
4. Sumo
5. Golf
6. Motor racing
7. Boxing
8. Pro wrestling

RUGBY IN JAPAN

OVERVIEW
Japan has the fourth largest number of rugby players the world: 125,000.

Rugby clubs: 3,631.

Rugby is the fifth most popular team sport (behind baseball, football, basketball and volleyball).

The national team, the Brave Blossoms, are ranked 11th in world.

Created in 2003, the most senior level of club rugby in Japan is called the Top League.

Highest attendance at a rugby match: 66,999 between Waseda University and Meiji University in 1952.

Since 2016 Japan has had a franchise, the Sunwolves, in the annual 18-team Super Rugby competition, which also features teams from Argentina, Australia, New Zealand and South Africa.

Numerous overseas star players who have played in the Top League including James Haskell (England), Sonny Bill Williams (New Zealand), Bernard Foley (Australia), Israel Folau (Australia) and Shane Williams (Wales).

Rugby clubs in Japan have mostly been organised by business corporations and even today most players are still classed as company employees.

HISTORY

The first rugby club in Japan, and Asia, was the Yokohama Football Club which started playing in 1866. The members and officers were Europeans and included alumni of Rugby School and Winchester College in England.

It is believed that the first Japanese players to participate in the sport were students at Keio University who were introduced to the game by Professor Edward Bramwell Clarke, born in Yokohama, and Ginnosuke Tanaka – both Cambridge University graduates. Clarke said that he wanted to give his students something constructive to do, as they 'seemed to have nothing to occupy them out of doors in the after-summer and after-winter days'.

Japanese rugby recovered quickly after World War II, and in September 1945, less than a month after the end of the war, an advertisement for rugby players in Hokkaido was placed. At the end of 1945, Kobe Steel encouraged its workers to play the game, setting a precedent for the later involvement of businesses in Japanese rugby.

GROWING PAINS

Rugby grew in popularity and participation in Japan during the 1970s and 80s, but this also led to issues around the game being fully amateur, something the game's officials were keen to uphold. Traditionally, many of their teams have been run by large corporations and the players were employees of these companies.

In the 1970s, large numbers of foreign players started playing in corporate teams and although technically amateurs, they were paid more for being employees than fellow workers. Japan was not alone, in this pre-professional, in blurring the line between amateurism and professionalism.

Former Australia and Japan player Ian Williams, who played for Kobe Steelers, estimated in 1994 that there were 100 foreigners playing rugby in Japan, receiving double the local wage, with few having 'real jobs'.

RUGBY TODAY

The professional Top League kicked off in 2003 featuring 12 teams, which grew to 14 in 2006 and then 16 in 2013. The Top League is played during the off-season of the Pacific-based, franchise league Super Rugby. In October 2012, Yokogawa Musashino forfeited four matches after one of their players taunted an opponent from a team affected by the year's earthquake and tsunami.

The most successful Top League teams are Toshiba Brave Lupus and Suntory Sungoliath, who have both won the title five times. The current champions are Kobelco Steelers. The Top League pays high salaries to world class foreign players and a small number of Japanese players, but most local-based players are still amateur. It was widely reported that in 2012, South African Jaque Fourie was paid $700,000 for a season by Kobelco Steelers in the Top League, making him the world's highest-paid player at the time.

The importance of the 2019 Rugby World Cup providing extra finance and publicity to the sport in Japan cannot be understated. Rugby in the whole of Asia is also expected to benefit, which is one of the reasons that Japan was chosen to host the tournament.

In 2002, Japan and South Korea jointly held the FIFA World Cup, which led to improved facilities and a spike in enthusiasm for that sport in those countries. Rugby in Japan and Asia will be looking for a similar boost.

As part of the build-up to the World Cup, and to help host cities stress test their venues and infrastructure, two matches of the 2019 World Rugby Pacific Nations Cup in July and August will be held in the country.

The Brave Blossoms will face Fiji in Kamaishi and Tonga in Hanazono.

CHAPTER 3
THE TOURNAMENT

HOW THE BID WAS WON

Japan will be the first country in Asia, and outside those who contest the Rugby Championship or Six Nations, to host a Rugby World Cup, having seen its bids for the two previous tournaments fail. Initially 10 unions had expressed an interest in hosting the World Cup, in either 2015 or 2019, to the International Rugby Board (IRB).

Russia bid for both tournaments but withdrew in February 2009 in favour of what proved to be a successful bid for the 2013 Rugby World Cup Sevens. Australia withdrew from the bidding process soon after, while Jamaica's early and surprising interest soon waned. Eventually, three potential hosts for 2019 – Italy, Japan and South Africa – were announced in May 2009.

At a meeting held at its headquarters in Dublin, the IRB confirmed that England would host the 2015 tournament and that Japan would be hosts four years later. The vote was 16–10 in favour.

"It's a dream for any rugby nation to host a World Cup," said Koji Tokumasu, the driving force behind Japan's successful bid.

I wanted to change Japan rugby and I thought if we were to bring the World Cup here, it could change everything," he told Wales Online.

"Rugby must go to all corners of the world, not just a very small part of it. The fact the World Cup is coming to Japan is very important. This isn't just a tournament for rugby, but for the whole of Japan and its people."

Tokumasu, who is also president of Asia Rugby, added: "Rugby is a very spiritual sport here and despite Japan having a very different culture to countries who have hosted the World Cup before, we want to celebrate that rather than follow the example set by other nations. If we try to westernise our tournament, it will not work here."

Japan's bid was not a shoo-in, though, amid concerns that the country was not fully equipped to manage the tournament. As late as 2015, Japan had to submit a revised plan after the Japanese government's decision to initially scrap Tokyo's National Stadium – an integral part of the bid – when the price tag balloned to $2 billion.

A remodelled National Stadium is now being built, and will be used for the 2020 Olympic Games, but will not be completed until after the Rugby World Cup has ended. The shortfall will be taken up by the Tokyo Stadium, which will host more matches plus the opening ceremony and opening match. The Yokohama Stadium will host the final. A World Rugby statement said: "The Tokyo Stadium will replace the new National Stadium within the inventory of 12 host venues the length and breadth of Japan."

World Rugby Chairman Bernard Lapasset added: "These are exciting, unprecedented times for Japan Rugby and this revised roadmap reinforces and reflects the shared vision and mission to deliver a Rugby World Cup that will be great for Japan, great for Asia and great for rugby."

THE VENUES

There have been numerous alterations to the venues submitted in the Japan RFU's original bid of 2009. (See where the different venues are located on the map of Japan at the end of the book.)

Venues in Hong Kong and Singapore have been withdrawn and all matches will now take place in Japan. The Chichibunomiya Stadium in Tokyo, owned by the Japan RFU, which might have been expected to host some games in the capital, is no longer on the list and the new National Stadium will not be built in time.

These are the 12 venues for the 2019 Rugby World Cup.

TOKYO STADIUM, CHOFU
(OPENED 2001, CAPACITY: 49,970)

This stadium, also known as the Ajinomoto Stadium, is in Chofu, in the Tokyo metropolitan area. It was the first stadium in Japan to offer naming rights, which were sold to the Ajinomoto company. The stadium is the home of J1 League football club FC Tokyo and J2 League club Tokyo Verdy, while also being used for rugby and American football. For the 2002 FIFA World Cup, Saudi Arabia used the stadium as a training ground, although it did not host a World Cup match. The north end of the stadium is adjacent to Chofu Airport, while Route 20 runs close to the south end where the main gate is situated.

Rugby World Cup 2019 fixtures at the stadium: Pool A - Japan v Russia (Sept 20); Pool C – Argentina v Tonga (Sept 28); Pool D – Georgia v Fiji (Oct 3); Pool C – USA v Tonga (Oct 13).

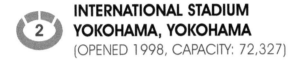

INTERNATIONAL STADIUM YOKOHAMA, YOKOHAMA
(OPENED 1998, CAPACITY: 72,327)

Yokohama's population of 3.7 million makes it Japan's largest city after the Tokyo special wards. It lies on Tokyo Bay, south of Tokyo, in the Kanto region of the main island of Honshu. The stadium, also called the Nissan Stadium, is the home of J1 League side Yokohama F Marinos. It has the highest capacity of any stadium in Japan, with 72,327 seats. It will host the 2019 Rugby World Cup semi-finals and final. It staged three first-round games during the 2002 FIFA World Cup, and the final between Germany and Brazil. The stadium is one of the planned football venues for the 2020 Olympics.

Rugby World Cup 2019 fixtures at the stadium: Pool B – New Zealand v South Africa (Sept 21); Pool A – Ireland v Scotland (Sept 22); Pool D - England v France (Oct 12); Pool C – Japan v Scotland (Oct 13); semi-finals (Oct 26 & 27); final (Nov 2).

3 SHIZUOKA STADIUM ECOPA, FUKUROI
(OPENED 2001, CAPACITY: 50,889)

Based in the modest coastal plain town of Fukuroi, 119 miles south of Tokyo, the Shizuoka Stadium Ecopa is the centrepiece of the larger Ogasayama Sports Park. Primarily used for football, the stadium is the main venue for major sporting events in Shizuoka Prefecture including athletics. It also played host to some matches during the 2002 FIFA World Cup, including Belgium versus Russia in the group stage (which Belgium won 3-2) and the quarter-final in which between Brazil beat England 2-1. Ecopa is the venue for more high-profile games of J-League side, Jubilo Iwata.

Rugby World Cup 2019 fixtures at the stadium: Pool A – Japan v Ireland (Sept 28); Pool A – Scotland v Russia (Oct 9); Pool B – South Africa v Italy (Oct 4); Pool D – Australia v Georgia (Oct 11).

4 HANAZONO RUGBY STADIUM, HIGASHIOSAKA
(OPENED 1929, CAPACITY: 30,000)

The oldest designated rugby arena in the country, the Hanazono Rugby Stadium is based in the town of Higashiosaka, near Osaka. This industrial town of more than 500,000 residents is in the heartland of the sport in Japan, hence its nickname of 'the rugby town'. The stadium is the home of the Kintetsu Liners rugby team and, in 2006, where Daisuke Ohata broke the world record for the overall number of test match tries with a hat-trick for Japan against Georgia. His total of 65, which he was later to increase to 69, saw him beat the previous record holder, David Campese from Australia. The stadium underwent a major renovation during 2017-18 in preparation for the Rugby World Cup.

Rugby World Cup 2019 fixtures at the stadium: Pool B – Italy v Namibia (Sept 22); Pool C – Argentina v Tonga (Sept 28); Pool D – Georgia v Fiji (Oct 3); Pool C – USA v Tonga (Oct 13).

CITY OF TOYOTA STADIUM, TOYOTA
(OPENED 2001, CAPACITY: 45,000)

The Toyota Stadium is in the town of Toyota, 16 miles outside the city of Nagoya, and is used by J-League team Nagoya Grampus and top-flight rugby side Toyota Verblitz. The stadium's main feature is its retractable roof, which folds like an accordion, although it has never been closed since 2015 because of maintenance costs. The longstanding ties between the Toyota Motor Corporation and the town of Toyota, formerly known as Koromo, gave the town its current name. It is the largest city in Japan which is not served by the national railway system.

Rugby World Cup 2019 fixtures at the stadium: Pool A – Japan v Samoa (Oct 5); Pool B – South Africa v Namibia (Sept 28); Pool B – New Zealand v Italy (Oct 12); Pool D – Wales v Georgia (Sept 23)

OITA STADIUM, OITA
(OPENED 2001, CAPACITY: 40,000)

The stadium is also known as the Oita Bank Dome and is a multi-purpose stadium in the city of Oita on Kyushu Island, the most south westerly of the country's four main islands. Three matches at the 2002 FIFA World Cup were held at the stadium including Senegal's 2-1 victory over Sweden in the round of 16. Since then, 3,000 temporary seats have been removed to allow access to the running track. It will play host to five matches in the Rugby World Cup. The city of Ōita has a humid subtropical climate which means it has hot summers and cool winters. Rainfall is significantly lower in winter.

Rugby World Cup 2019 fixtures at the stadium: Pool B – New Zealand v Canada (Oct 2); Pool D – Australia v Uruguay (Oct 5); Pool D – Wales v Fiji (Oct 9); quarter-finals (Oct 19 & 20).

 ### KAMAISHI RECOVERY MEMORIAL STADIUM, KAMAISHI
(OPENED 2018, CAPACITY: 16,187)

The Kamaishi Recovery Memorial Stadium, also known as Kamaishi Unosumai Stadium, was completed in 2018 and built specifically for the Rugby World Cup. The stadium will use an additional 10,000 temporary seats for the competition, with 6,000 permanent seats remaining after the tournament. It has been built on the site of schools which were destroyed by the earthquake and tsunami, which hit the city of Kamaishi in 2011, leaving more than 1,000 residents dead or missing. Kamaishi is a city of just under 35,000 residents, located on the rugged Sanrika coast in Iwate Prefecture, 337 miles north of Tokyo.

Rugby World Cup 2019 fixtures at the stadium: Pool C – Fiji v Uruguay (Sept 25); Pool B – Namibia v Canada (Oct 13).

 KUMAGAYA RUGBY STADIUM, KUMAGAYA
(OPENED 1991, CAPACITY: 30,000)

Used mostly for rugby matches, the stadium was built in 1991 and renovated between 2016 and 2018, expanding its capacity from 20,000 (10,000 seated) to 24,000 (fully seated). Another 600 temporary seats will be added for the two Rugby World Cup matches to be played at the venue. It is the home stadium of senior rugby team Panasonic Wild Knights. The city of Kumagaya has a humid subtropical climate and a reputation as one of the hottest areas in Japan in summer. In 2007, the city recorded 40.9 °C (105.6 °F), breaking the 74-year record for the highest temperature in Japan. Temperatures in late September and early October, when the World Cup matches will take place, are expected to be a more pleasant 20 °C (68 °F) although rainfall and humidity may still be high.

Rugby World Cup 2019 fixtures at the stadium: Pool A – Russia v Samoa (Sept 24); Pool D – Georgia v Uruguay (Sept 29); Pool C – Argentina v USA (Oct 9).

KOBE MISAKI STADIUM, KOBE
(OPENED 2001, CAPACITY: 30,132)

Also called the Noevir Stadium Kobe, the venue is in Misaki Park, Hyogo-ku, Kobe and has a capacity of 30,132. This stadium, which features a retractable roof, is home to J1 League club Vissel Kobe and rugby side Kobelco Steelers. In order to host three 2002 FIFA World Cup matches, the stadium was renovated to install a removable roof and increase spectator capacity to 42,000. Kobe city is located on the southern side of the main island of Honshu, on the north shore of Osaka Bay, about 19 miles west of Osaka. Wedged between the coast and the mountains, the port city of Kobe is long and narrow and has given its name to Kobe beef, a type of Wagyu beef which is a delicacy around the world.

Rugby World Cup 2019 fixtures at the stadium: Pool A – Scotland v Samoa (Sept 30); Pool A – Ireland v Russia (Oct 3); Pool C – England v USA (Sept 26).

KUMAMOTO STADIUM, KUMAMOTA
(OPENED 1998, CAPACITY: 32,000)

This multi-purpose stadium, also known as the Egao Kenko Stadium, is based in the east ward of the city of Kumamota, on the island of Kyushu, and is the southernmost venue in the Rugby World Cup. The venue is currently used by J-League 2 football team Roasso Kumamoto and occasionally for Top League rugby matches. The city of Kumamoto is an amalgamation of numerous smaller towns. It is in a sub-tropical zone, and in 2016 an earthquake tremor of 7.1 was recorded on the Moment Magnitude Scale. The tradition of eating basashi (raw horse meat) originated here and remains popular, although now it is usually considered a delicacy. The practice began during the 1877 Satsuma Rebellion when Kumamoto Castle was besieged for 53 days.

Rugby World Cup 2019 fixtures at the stadium: Pool C – France v Tonga (Oct 6); Pool D – Wales v Uruguay (Oct 13).

SAPPORO DOME, SAPPORO
(OPENED 2001, CAPACITY: 41,410)

Sapporo Dome is home of pro baseball team Hokkaido Nippon-Ham Fighters and football club Hokkaido Consadole Sapporo, and is one of the planned football venues for the 2020 Olympics. This stadium hosted three matches during the 2002 FIFA World Cup and made history as the first venue where both indoor and night time skiing events took place on a World Championship or Winter Olympic Games level. In 2009, renovations were made to the Dome allowing for the possibility of increasing the capacity to 53,796 on a temporary basis. The main feature of the Dome is its retractable surface. Baseball is currently played on an underlying artificial turf field, and football takes place on a grass pitch which slides in and out of the stadium. The city of Soppora has the fifth largest population in Japan and is the largest city on the island of Hokkaido. Sapporo, which hosted the 1972 Winter Olympics, is the northernmost city used at the Rugby World Cup.

Rugby World Cup 2019 fixtures at the stadium: Pool D – Australia v Fiji (Sept 21); Pool C – England v Tonga (Sept 22).

FUKUOKA HAKATANOMORI STADIUM, FUKUOKA,
(OPENED 1995, CAPACITY: 22,563)

The stadium, also known as the Level 5 Stadium, is home to the Avispa Fukuoka football club, while also hosting Top League and international rugby matches. It is a 20-minute walk or a short bus ride from Fukuoka Airport. The city was formed when Hakata and Fukuoka merged in 1889. At a meeting, it was agreed that the city would be called Hakata; however, a group of samurai forced those present at the meeting to choose Fukuoka. The city is the economic centre of the Kyushu region, largely focused on the service sector, and the only economic zone for business start-ups.

Rugby World Cup 2019 fixtures at the stadium: Pool B – Italy v Canada (Sept 26); Pool C – France v USA (Oct 2); Pool A – Ireland v Samoa (Oct 12).

QUALIFICATION

The teams which finished in the top three places in each of the four pools at the 2015 Rugby World Cup automatically qualified for the 2019 tournament. One of these 12 teams was Japan, who finished third in Pool B in 2015. However, as the hosts, they were already assured of their place. The remaining eight spaces were decided by existing regional competitions around the world, followed by numerous cross regional play-offs. The final spot was decided by a four-team repechage tournament in France in November 2018, which was won by Canada.

A total of 93 teams originally took part in the qualifying procedure for the 2019 Rugby World Cup, the first match being when Jamaica beat Saint Vincent and the Grenadines 48-0 on March 5, 2016, just five months after the 2015 final.

HOW THE TEAMS QUALIFIED

Automatically: South Africa, England, France, Georgia, Ireland, Italy, Scotland, Wales, Australia, New Zealand, Argentina, Japan.

Regional qualifiers: Namibia (Africa), USA (Americas), Russia (Europe), Fiji (Oceania 1), Tonga (Oceania 2), Uruguay (Americas 2).

Regional play-offs: Samoa.

Repechage final: Canada.

QUALIFICATION CONTROVERSY

Russia replaced Romania in the 2019 Rugby World Cup finals after an independent committee decided that Romania, along with Spain and Belgium, had repeatedly fielded ineligible players in the Rugby Europe Championship. The teams were docked points and given hefty suspended fines; Belgium 30 points and £125,000, Spain 40 points and £30,000, and Romania 30 points and £100,000.

The qualification process had already seen controversy when in-form Spain lost 18-10 to Belgium in the final round of the Championship. Much to the Spanish team's displeasure, the match was overseen by three Romanian officials. The referee was escorted from the field after the result, which initially handed Romania a World Cup place before they were docked points. Five Spain players were later suspended for between 14 and 43 weeks for their parts in the disturbance at the end of the match.

Germany also benefited from the decision to dock Romania points, allowing them to reach the Europe play-offs, where they beat Portugal, before losing in the regional play-offs to Samoa and eventually to Canada in the repechage tournament.

REPECHAGE QUALIFICATION

Canada secured the last place in the World Cup after being triumphant in the round-robin repechage final tournament in France, overcoming second-placed Germany, and Hong Kong and Kenya, who were third and fourth respectively. It had been a surprise that the Canucks had failed to qualify automatically through the Americas regional tournament, but they made amends by beating Kenya 65-19, Germany 29-10 and Hong Kong 27-10 in the repechage.

Victory maintains their record of having featured in every Rugby World Cup finals tournament since its inception in 1987.

THE DRAW

The draw for the pool stages of the 2019 Rugby World Cup finals occurred in the Japanese city of Kyoto on May 10, 2017.

The draw is traditionally made during December in the year following the previous World Cup, after the November internationals, but it was pushed back allowing teams to enjoy a longer period to improve their world rankings ahead of the draw.

The four pools of five teams were drawn randomly with the 12 automatic qualifiers from 2015 allocated to their respective bands (one, two and three based on their world rankings), and the remaining two bands made up of the eight qualifying teams, with allocation to each band being based on form at the previous Rugby World Cup.

Band 1 teams: Ireland, New Zealand, England, Australia.
Band 2 teams: Scotland, South Africa, France, Wales.
Band 3 teams: Japan, Italy, Argentina, Georgia.
Band 4 teams: Russia, Namibia, USA, Fiji.
Band 5 teams: Samoa, Canada, Tonga, Uruguay.

The draw opened with Japanese Prime Minister Shinzo Abe drawing the pool where Japan would be allocated, which was Pool A, after which the draw continued starting with Band 5 teams.

THE POOLS

Pool A: Ireland, Scotland, Japan, Russia, Samoa.

Pool B: New Zealand, South Africa, Italy, Namibia, Canada.

Pool C: England, France, Argentina, USA, Tonga.

Pool D: Australia, Wales, Georgia, Fiji, Uruguay.

HOW THE POOLS WORK

Each round-robin pool consists of 10 matches in which each team plays each other once. Teams are awarded four points for a win, two for a draw and none for a defeat by eight or more points.

Teams can also earn a crucial bonus point by scoring four tries in a match, or by losing by fewer than eight points. Two bonus points are awarded if both situations apply.

If two or more teams are tied on match points, tie-breakers apply, starting with the winner of the match between the two teams and then the difference between points scored for and against in all pool matches.

The teams finishing in the top two of each pool advance to the quarter-finals. The top three teams of each pool receive automatic qualification to the 2023 Rugby World Cup in France.

WHAT TO EXPECT IN THE POOLS

POOL A
Ireland, Scotland, Japan, Russia, Samoa

EXPECTATIONS
At the end of 2018, in-form Ireland were seen many seasoned rugby-watchers as joint favourites to lift the Webb Ellis Cup this year. Their task was to maintain the high expectations, which have built up around the squad in the previous two years. During that time, they won the Six Nations championship and twice beat New Zealand, the No.1 ranked nation in the world.

However, a sub-standard performance in the 2019 Six Nations has caused some to doubt Ireland's World Cup-winning credentials. As the world-ranked No.3 rugby team, Ireland are not expected to face many issues in the pool and should win it.

An unpredictable Scotland, after finishing fifth in the Six Nations and losing 22-13 at home to Ireland, will be expected to finish in the runners-up place, progressing to the quarter-finals alongside the Irish.

But this is a well-matched pool, which should throw up at least one surprise result. The real interest in this pool is the lower ranked teams, of which hosts Japan will be heavily scrutinised. Following the memorable victory over South Africa in the 2015 Rugby World Cup, pressure will be on the Brave Blossoms to at least finish third in the pool, ensuring a place in the tournament in four years' time. However, buoyed by what should be impressive home support, they will be focusing on a top-two finish and a place in the knockout stages.

Russia are the minnows of the pool, and it would be a major surprise for them to win a match while Samoa, despite needing to win the regional play-offs to reach the tournament, are always an aggressive, physically threatening team and could cause an upset.

Bonus points could be key in this pool.

THE MATCHES TO WATCH

The result of the Ireland versus Scotland match on September 22 should determine the winner of the group. The pressure on both European teams to perform could produce a tense, exciting encounter which might effectively be a title decider. Another match to savour will be on October 13 when Scotland faces Japan in the final pool game, the result of which could determine which team finishes as runners-up.

POTENTIAL UPSET

A win for a fired-up Samoa over Scotland on September 30 is not out of the question, particularly this early in the tournament. It would probably leave both teams and Japan scrapping over second place.

POOL A MATCHES

Japan ____ – ____ Russia

Friday, September 20 at Tokyo Stadium, ko 7.45pm (GMT 10.45am)

Ireland ____ – ____ Scotland

Sunday, September 22 at International Stadium Yokohama, ko 4.45pm (GMT 7.45am)

Russia ____ – ____ Samoa

Tuesday, September 24 at Kumagaya Rugby Stadium, ko 7.15pm (GMT 10.15am)

Japan ____ – ____ Ireland

Saturday, September 28 at Shizuoka Stadium Ecopa, ko 4.15pm (GMT 7.15am)

Scotland ____ – ____ Samoa

Monday, September 30 at Kobe Misaki Stadium, ko 7.15pm (GMT 10.15am)

Ireland ____ – ____ Russia

Thursday, October 3 at Kobe Misaki Stadium, ko 7.15pm (GMT 10.15)

Japan ____ – ____ Samoa

Saturday, October 5 at City of Toyota Stadium, ko 7.30pm (GMT 10.30am)

Scotland ____ – ____ Russia

Wednesday, October 9 at Shizuoka Stadium, ko 4.15pm (GMT 7.15am)

Ireland _____ – _____ **Samoa**

Saturday, October 12 at Fukuoka Stadium, ko 7.45pm (GMT 10.45am)

Japan _____ – _____ **Scotland**

Sunday, October 13 at International Stadium Yokohama, ko 7.45pm (GMT 10.45am)

HOW POOL A FINISHED

1. _____ **Pts** _____

2. _____ **Pts** _____

3. _____ **Pts** _____

4. _____ **Pts** _____

5. _____ **Pts** _____

REMEMBER

The winner of Pool A will face the runners-up of Pool B, and vice versa, in the quarter-finals.

POOL B
New Zealand, South Africa, Italy, Namibia, Canada

EXPECTATIONS
This pool looks more straight forward than any other, especially when assessing which two teams will finish first and second.

World No.1 team New Zealand are strong favourites to claim top spot, given their form and the fact that they are the most consistent and successful nation in Rugby World Cup history. If they are to lose a match, it can surely only be to South Africa, who have been going through a rebuilding phase under new head coach Rassie Erasmus, and who beat the All Blacks 36-34 in the Rugby Championship in Wellington in September 2018.

This pool contains two African teams with Namibia reaching their fifth consecutive finals, after having won their regional group. They are an improving side but their only realistic chance of a victory will come against Canada, and even that might be a stretch.

Italy will be expected to take third place in the table as a Tier 1 nation, but they have often under-performed in the finals, while Canada, despite only scraping through, are an experienced World Cup team.

THE MATCHES TO WATCH
Set your alarm for the pool opener at Yokohama on September 22, when three-time champions New Zealand face two-time winners South Africa. The successful side will almost certainly top the pool, so expect the contest to be a no-nonsense affair with neither team holding anything in reserve for later matches.

Neither side will want to finish second in the pool and most likely face Ireland in the quarter-finals. However, you don't want to overlook Italy versus Canada on September 26, which should be a romp for the European side but, coming just four days after their clash with Namibia, may be more of a challenge than first appears.

POTENTIAL UPSET

Can Italy recapture the form which saw them unexpectedly beat South Africa for the first time in November 2016? It's unlikely that they can repeat that 20-18 score line, but the Springboks were humbled by Japan at the 2015 Rugby World Cup, so slipping up against lower ranked opposition is not unknown to them.

Remember, Italy are a Tier 1 nation and will probably come into the match off the back of two comfortable victories, so will have confidence on their side.

POOL B MATCHES

New Zealand _____ – _____ South Africa
Saturday, September 21 at International Stadium Yokohama, ko 6.45pm (GMT 9.45am)

Italy _____ – _____ Namibia
Sunday, September 22 at Hanazono Rugby Stadium, ko 2.15pm (GMT 5.15am)

Italy _____ – _____ Canada
Thursday, September 26 at Fukuoka Hakatanomori Stadium, ko 4.45pm (GMT 7.45am)

South Africa _____ – _____ Namibia
Saturday, September 28 at City of Toyota Stadium, ko 6.45pm (GMT 9.45am)

New Zealand _____ – _____ Canada
Wednesday, October 2, at Oita Stadium, ko 7.15pm (GMT 10.15am)

South Africa _____ – _____ Italy
Friday, October 4 at Shizuoka Stadium, ko 6.45pm (GMT 9.45am)

New Zealand _____ – _____ Namibia
Sunday, October 6 at Tokyo Stadium, ko 1.45pm (GMT 4.45am)

South Africa _____ – _____ Canada
Tuesday, October 8 at Kobe Misaki Stadium, ko 7.15pm (GMT 10.15am)

New Zealand _____ – _____ Italy

Saturday, October 12 at City of Toyota Stadium, ko 1.45pm (GMT 4.45am)

Namibia _____ – _____ Canada

Sunday, October 13 at Kamaishi Recovery Memorial Stadium, ko 12.15pm (GMT 3.15am)

HOW POOL B FINISHED

1. _____ Pts _____

2. _____ Pts _____

3. _____ Pts _____

4. _____ Pts _____

5. _____ Pts _____

REMEMBER

The winner of Pool B will face the runners-up of Pool A, and vice versa, in the quarter-finals.

POOL C
England, France, Argentina, USA, Tonga

EXPECTATIONS
Expect the unexpected in this pool which contains three Tier 1 nations in England, France and Argentina. It also has an improving USA side under Coach Gary Gold, and a Tonga side which, like most Pacific rugby nations, are a physical challenge and who like nothing better than leaving their mark on senior opponents.

England will be expected to top the pool having finished second in the Six Nations, overwhelming France 44-8 in doing so. However, they are susceptible, as proved in the match against Scotland in March when they drew 38-38, despite having led comfortably at half-time.

France are the likely runners-up, but are gloriously unpredictable, often finding a way to succeed in the tournament, while Argentina have been semi-finalists in two of last three World Cups and will not lack confidence. They could be the spanner in the works of England or France.

Tonga and the USA will be expected to struggle, with their head-to-head encounter being both teams' best opportunity to notch a victory.

THE MATCHES TO WATCH
France versus Argentina could be the most interesting contest of the pool as Gallic flair and ingenuity meets South American

power and drive head on. France at their best should win, but who knows whether they will be a unified force for that opening match of Pool C on September 21. The international Stadium Yokohama will feature England versus France on October 12 in what will be both teams' final pool match, and one which might determine who finishes top of the pile.

POTENTIAL UPSET

The long shot of a Pool C upset could come when France meet Tonga just four days after having played the USA. The French will have rested players and will use their squad wisely in the run-up. However, meeting a physical side like Tonga after such a short turnaround will test all their faculties.

Tonga will be keen to inflict a bloody nose on a Tier 1 team and will have enjoyed a week's break to focus their attention. It would be a result to match Japan's victory over South Africa from four years ago.

POOL C MATCHES

France ____ – ____ Argentina
Saturday, September 21 at Tokyo Stadium, ko 4.15pm (GMT 7.15am)

England ____ – ____ Tonga
Sunday, September 22 at Sapporo Dome, ko 7.15pm (GMT 10.15am)

England ____ – ____ USA
Thursday, September 26 at Kobe Misaki Stadium, ko 7.45pm (GMT 10.45am)

Argentina ____ – ____ Tonga
Saturday, September 28 at Hanazono Rugby Stadium, ko 1.45pm (GMT 4.45am)

France ____ – ____ USA
Wednesday, October 2, at Fukuoka Hakatanomori Stadium, ko 4.45pm (GMT 7.45am)

England ____ – ____ Argentina
Saturday, October 5 at Tokyo Stadium, ko 5.00pm (GMT 8.00am)

France ____ – ____ Tonga
Sunday, October 6 at Kumamoto Stadium, ko 4.45pm (GMT 7.45am)

Argentina ____ – ____ USA
Wednesday, October 9 at Kumagaya Rugby Stadium, ko 1.45pm (GMT 4.45am)

England _____ – _____ France

Saturday, October 12 at International Stadium Yokohama, ko 5.15pm (GMT 8.15am)

USA _____ – _____ Tonga

Sunday, October 13 at Hanazono Rugby Stadium, ko 2.45pm (GMT 5.45am)

HOW POOL C FINISHED

1. _____ Pts _____

2. _____ Pts _____

3. _____ Pts _____

4. _____ Pts _____

5. _____ Pts _____

REMEMBER

The winner of Pool C will face the runners-up of Pool D, and vice versa, in the quarter-finals.

POOL D
Australia, Wales, Georgia, Fiji, Uruguay

EXPECTATIONS

Pool D looks likely to be the most lively and entertaining pool of the World Cup and one where four teams, all ranked among the top 12 teams in the world, will feel they have a route to the knockout stage. Relative minnows Uruguay will, however, have to work hard to avoid four substantial defeats.

Australia, Wales, Fiji and Uruguay were also drawn together in the same pool four years ago. World No.2 ranked team Wales are favourites to finish top, especially after their impressive Grand Slam performance in the 2019 Six Nations championship, whereas an inconsistent Australia should take the runners-up spot.

Fiji are ranked No.9 in the world – easily the highest ranked Tier 2 team – and remain one of the most entertaining and dynamic teams in the sport. They will pounce on any weaknesses shown by the two senior teams. Given the Wallabies' recent form, the Fijians will back themselves to come second in the pool and move into the knockout stage for the first time since 2007.

Georgia are world-ranked No.12 and the best Tier 2 team in Europe. They will expect to beat Uruguay and focus on their structured game plan to overturn error-prone Fiji, although the last time the two teams met in 2018 the Pacific Islanders won 37-15.

Uruguay, the weakest team in the group, ranked a respectable 16th in the world, could find themselves the whipping boys of the pool.

THE MATCHES TO WATCH

Wales versus Fiji will be one to savour. It will pit Wales, the most in-form and confident nation in world rugby, against a Fiji team playing their final pool match, and possibly needing to win to progress into the next stage. Wales might well be content to match Fiji in all departments of the game leading to a thrilling, high scoring contest.

These two nations have met in the pool stage of the last three World Cups with Fiji winning 38-34 in 2007, while Wales won 66-0 in 2011 and 23-13 in 2015. Expect fireworks. The clash between Australia and Wales is also one to watch as it should decide who finishes top and should be close, if their 15-6 contest in the 2015 World Cup is a measure.

POTENTIAL UPSET

Whether Fiji, world-ranked No.9, beating Australia, world-ranked No.6, can be classed as a shock is up for debate, but it would certainly be a surprise and blow the pool wide open. It is the opening match of the pool, and defeat for either side will seriously put into doubt their chances of progressing into the quarter-finals. Nerves will be on show, but this is what makes it a more even contest. Four years ago, the Wallabies won 28-13, but the gap between the teams has shrunk since then.

POOL D MATCHES

Australia _____ – _____ **Fiji**
Saturday, September 21 at Sapporo Dome, ko 1.45pm (GMT 4.45am)

Wales _____ – _____ **Georgia**
Monday, September 23 at City of Toyota Stadium, ko 7.15pm (GMT 10.15am)

Fiji _____ – _____ **Uruguay**
Wednesday, September 25 at Kamaishi Recovery Memorial Stadium, ko 2.15pm (GMT 5.15am)

Georgia _____ – _____ **Uruguay**
Sunday, September 29 at Kumagaya Rugby Stadium, ko 2.15pm (GMT 5.15am)

Australia _____ – _____ **Wales**
Sunday, September 29, at Tokyo Stadium, ko 4.45pm (GMT 7.45am)

Georgia _____ – _____ **Fiji**
Thursday, October 3 at Hanazono Rugby Stadium, ko 2.15pm (GMT 5.15am)

Australia _____ – _____ **Uruguay**
Saturday, October 5 at Oita Stadium, ko 2.15pm (GMT 5.15am)

Wales _____ – _____ **Fiji**
Wednesday, October 9 at Oita Stadium, ko 6.45pm (GMT 9.45am)

Australia _____ – _____ **Georgia**
Friday, October 11 at Shizuoka Stadium, ko 7.15pm (GMT 10.15am)

Wales _____ – _____ **Uruguay**
Sunday, October 13 at Kumamoto Stadium, ko 5.15pm (GMT 8.15am)

HOW POOL D FINISHED

1. _____ Pts _____

2. _____ Pts _____

3. _____ Pts _____

4. _____ Pts _____

5. _____ Pts _____

REMEMBER

The winner of Pool D will face the runners-up of Pool C, and vice versa, in the quarter-finals.

KNOCKOUT STAGE

After the pool stages have been completed, the top two teams in each of the four pools will progress to the quarter-finals which are played on a knockout basis. **There is a blank bracket for the knockout stage located at back of the book.**

The winners will advance to the semi-finals, and then the winners of those matches will head to the final while the losers will face-off in the bronze medal match.

Quarter-finals

QF No.1
Winner of Pool C v Runner-up of Pool D
Saturday, October 19 at Oita Stadium, ko 4.15pm (GMT 7.15am)

QF No.2
Winner of Pool B v Runner-up of Pool A
Saturday, October 19 at Tokyo Stadium, ko 7.15pm (GMT 10.15am)

QF No.3
Winner of Pool D v Runner-up of Pool C
Sunday, October 20 at Oita Stadium, ko 4.15pm (GMT 7.15)

QF No.4
Winner of Pool A v Runner-up of Pool B
Sunday, October 20 at Tokyo Stadium, ko 7.15pm (GMT 10.15am)

Semi-finals

SF No.1
Winner of QF No.1 v Winner of QF No.2
Saturday, October 26 at International Stadium Yokohama, ko
5.00pm (GMT 8.00am)

SF No.2
Winner of QF No.3 v Winner of QF No.4
Sunday, October 27 at International Stadium Yokohama, ko
6.00pm (GMT 9.00am)

Bronze medal match

Loser of SF No.1 v Loser of SF No.2
Friday, November 1 at Tokyo Stadium, ko 6.00pm (GMT 9.00am)

Final

Winner of SF No.1 v Winner of SF No.2
Saturday, November 2 at International Stadium Yokohama, ko
6.00pm (GMT 9.00am)

CHAPTER 4
THE TEAMS

OVERVIEW

A total of 20 teams have qualified for the 2019 Rugby World Cup, and each have been placed in one of four pools, depending upon their world ranking and placing at the 2015 Rugby World Cup.

Pool A: Ireland, Scotland, Japan, Russia, Samoa.

Pool B: New Zealand, South Africa, Italy, Namibia, Canada.

Pool C: England, France, Argentina, USA, Tonga.

Pool D: Australia, Wales, Georgia, Fiji, Uruguay.

In this chapter, the teams are described in detail in pool order, their expectations highlighted, strengths and weaknesses scrutinised and star players profiled.

IRELAND

FACTS

Nickname: None
World ranking: 3
Qualification: Automatic (Pool D winners in RWC 2015)
World Cup record: P 36, W 22, D 0, L 14
Biggest World Cup win: 64-7 against Namibia (2003)
Biggest World Cup defeat: 43-19 by New Zealand (1995) & 36-12 by France (1995)
World Cups – 8
Performances: Quarter-finals – 6, quarter-final play-offs – 1, pool stage – 1

RUGBY WORLD CUP HISTORY

In common with most Northern Hemisphere teams, Ireland have flattered only to deceive at World Cups. They have threatened to punch above their weight several times, but rarely succeeded.

To highlight their inconsistency over the years, Ireland have won two matches by a single point but also lost two matches by the same margin. They have played in all eight World Cup tournaments since the first in 1987 and topped their pool twice.

Ireland have qualified for the quarter-finals in all but two, however that has always been where their story ends. Their most disappointing tournament came in 2007 when they failed to progress from Pool D. They lost 30-15 to surprise pool winners Argentina and went down 25-5 to hosts France who took second place. Their lack of form in the tournament was highlighted with underwhelming victories over Georgia (14-10), and lowly-ranked Namibia (32-17).

Ireland came closest to reaching the semi-finals for the first time in 1991 when they lost a memorable match with Australia 19-18 at Lansdowne Road, Dublin. Gordon Hamilton put the Irish 18-15 ahead with six minutes remaining, but Michael Lynagh scored a last-gasp try to earn the Wallabies victory. Australia would go on to lift the Webb Ellis Cup after beating hosts England 12-6 in the final.

In 2015, Argentina knocked Ireland out of the tournament in the quarter-finals with a solid 43-20 victory.

BUILD-UP TO 2019 RUGBY WORLD CUP

In the 2018 Autumn Internationals, Ireland won all four of their matches for the second successive season, one of which was a historic 16-9 victory over New Zealand. This first ever victory over the All Blacks in Ireland led to New Zealand coach Steve Hansen cheekily labelling the Irish as the 'No.1 team in the world'.

They were also comfortable 54-7 winners over Italy at Soccer Field in Chicago – a venue where they had previously beaten the All Blacks in 2017 – and, back on home soil, they overcame Argentina 28-17 and the USA 57-14.

In November 2018, at the World Rugby awards, Joe Schmidt was named coach of the year and Johnny Sexton player of the year, in addition to Ireland scooping the team award. This memorable end to 2018 put them in good stead for the challenge of defending their Six Nations crown three months later.

However, this did not go as planned because Ireland were beaten easily by England and Wales leading to them eventually finishing the championship in third place. It was a disappointing defence of their crown, stalling the momentum which they had built up during the previous year.

Ireland have not become a poor team in the space of a few months, but the concern is that they peaked too soon and have now lost their mojo. They still possess classy players but will be looking for an injection of energy in all areas of their game, ahead of the World Cup.

In August and early September, Ireland have scheduled World Cup warm-up matches at home to Italy and Wales, and away to England and Wales.

HEAD COACH

New Zealand-born **Joe Schmidt** has overseen the most successful period in the Irish team's history since taking up the reins in 2013 but has plenty to occupy his mind after a demoralising Six Nations championship.

Ireland had gone from eighth in the world rankings to No.2 under his guidance, although they're now No.3, and have also beaten New Zealand, something that they had never achieved. In addition to these wins over the All Blacks in 2016 and 2018, Schmidt has steered Ireland to three Six Nations titles – including a Grand Slam - and a series win in Australia.

The 54-year-old, who since 2015 has dual New Zealand and Ireland citizenship, won the World Rugby coach of the year award in November 2018 after which he announced he would be leaving his role as head coach at the end of the World Cup in order to focus on his family commitments.

Ireland defensive coach Andy Farrell will be his replacement.

PLAYERS TO WATCH

Rory Best is the most successful Ireland captain ever and, at the age of 37, leads the team in a quiet and intelligent manner. He is the country's most capped hooker, with more than 120 caps, and has suggested that he will end his international playing days at the World Cup, a career which will have lasted 14 seasons.

Teammate Jonny Sexton has said that Best always puts the team first, adding: "He inspires you with the way he plays and how he speaks, but his decision making under pressure is his greatest strength as a captain."

Best is still setting himself goals and said: "The last two things would be to captain Ireland at a World Cup and then to win a quarter-final, they are the two big things that I have never done before."

His successful partnership with head coach Schmidt is one of the core strengths of this Ireland team.

If Rory Best is the team's rock, then **Johnny Sexton** is their talisman, a truly world class, match-winning fly-half. The 2018 World Rugby player of the year, Sexton starred as Ireland completed a Six Nations Grand Slam in 2018, scoring 44 points, and memorably slotting the crucial drop goal that ensured victory over France.

Sexton, 34, in conjunction with half-back partner **Conor Murray**, so often provides the quality Ireland need when facing the best teams in the world. His strength in defence and accurate passing, make him a considerable all-rounder, while his place and out-of-hand kicking is often faultless. His standards slipped in the 2019 Six Nations championship, which will be a concern to all Ireland fans.

If Sexton performs, so does Ireland.

The exciting **Joey Carbery** is seen as Sexton's long-term replacement at fly-half, however he is already a force to be reckoned with and would command a starting place in most international teams. The 23-year-old, who was born in New Zealand to Irish parents, is agile in attack and ferocious in defence, and although he has replaced Sexton during matches, his slight lack of consistency means he currently remains in the shadow of his former Leinster colleague. If he is given enough game time, the World Cup should be the perfect platform for him to showcase his undoubted talents, especially if Sexton fails to perform.

Jacob Stockdale is a flying winger who knows how to score tries, it is what he does best. The 23-year-old has always been on the Ireland radar and was marked out as a player of quality in his early days in Northern Ireland. The Ulsterman gained selection for the Ireland team in 2017, scoring a try on debut against South Africa. He stamped his name on the world stage in 2018 when he scored seven tries in Ireland's successful Six Nations Grand Slam campaign, creating a new record for the tournament. His try-scoring record is 14 tries in 19 tests, which, if Ireland are successful, he will be expected to build upon in Japan.

Don't overlook: **Peter O'Mahony**, the Munster back row who is the team's Mr Consistent, and **Keith Earls**, a match-winning winger with more than 75 caps.

TEAM STYLE

Ireland are in the most successful period in their rugby history, beating all before them from the Northern and Southern Hemispheres in the last two years. Yet their style, which England coach Eddie Jones mischievously labelled 'kick and clap,' is considered by some to be over-reliant on the tactical kicking game.

Their 32-20 defeat at home to England at the start of the 2019 Six Nations saw critics scrutinise their one-dimensional style again. But Captain Rory Best has been quoted as saying that it was a 'lack of kicking accuracy and physicality' that cost them.

Ireland are unlikely to change the style which has made them so successful, but they will need a defined alternative set of tactics if their go-to game plan doesn't work. However, they have the strength in their squad to do this and have proved, under boss Joe Schmidt, that they can take on new ideas and tactics. Their capitulation to Wales in March and the uncharacteristically high number of errors they made, even in previously strong areas like the restarts, is a concern.

EXPECTATIONS

There is no question that expectations of a successful World Cup were high at the end of 2018, perhaps too high, particularly of a team which is yet to reach the semi-finals after eight attempts. But perhaps now they can come into the tournament without the spotlight being on them, the tag of being potential winners having slightly faded.

Any pressure on their shoulders will come from trying to regroup and find their form, rather than being favourites. This might suit them. Don't underestimate Ireland's ability and desire to bounce back, they have not become a bad team overnight.

PREDICTION

Irish eyes will stop smiling in the semi-finals.

IRELAND'S POOL A FIXTURES

Scotland: Sunday, September 22 at International Stadium Yokohama, ko 4.45pm (GMT 7.45am)

Japan: Saturday, September 28 at Shizuoka Stadium, ko 4.15pm (GMT 7.15am)

Russia: Thursday, October 3 at Kobe Misaki Stadium, ko 7.15pm (GMT 10.15)

Samoa: Saturday, October 12 at Fukuoka Stadium, ko 7.45pm (10.45am)

SCOTLAND

FACTS

Nickname: None
World ranking: 7
Qualification: Automatic (Pool B runners-up in RWC 2015)
World Cup record: P 39, W 23, D 1, L 15
Biggest World Cup win: 69-0 against Ivory Coast (1995)
Biggest World Cup defeat: 51-9 by France (2003)
World Cups – 8
Performances: Third-place play-off – 1, quarter-finals – 6, pool stage – 1.

RUGBY WORLD CUP HISTORY

The quarter-finals have been where Scotland's World Cup dreams have usually ended, having been knocked out at this stage in six of their eight tournaments.

The Scots began their World Cup history with a memorable 20-20 draw against France in 1987, and four years later they enjoyed their most successful tournament when they reached the third-place play-off against New Zealand, a match they narrowly lost 13-6. That year, they topped their pool after beating Japan (47-9), Zimbabwe (51-12) and Ireland (24-15), before downing Western Samoa 28-6 in the quarter-finals. However, their campaign ended with back-to-back defeats; a tight 9-6 setback to England in the semi-final and then the defeat in the third-place play-off to the All Blacks.

The Scots have never been able to raise their game to such lofty levels again, often disposing of more junior opponents with ease in the pool stages, before failing to overcome more senior opposition. However, they have come so close.

In 2011, under head coach Andy Robinson, Scotland suffered their worst, and most frustrating, tournament when they failed to escape the pool stage for the only time in their history. Unimpressive wins over Romania and Georgia were followed by agonising defeats to Argentina (13-12) and England (16-12), both thrillers which could have gone either way.

Their campaign in 2015 saw them finish second in the pool after a nervy 36-33 win over Samoa but ended in the quarter-finals in agonising fashion again. This time they lost 35-34 to Australia at Twickenham after conceding a late, controversial penalty.

BUILD-UP TO 2019 RUGBY WORLD CUP

Scotland won two and lost two matches during their 2018 Autumn Internationals beginning with a 21-10 setback to Wales in Cardiff. This was followed by a convincing 54-17 victory over the visiting Fijians before two tight matches.

South Africa visited a packed Murrayfield and edged out a determined Scotland team 26-20 with fly-half Handre Pollard scoring 18 points.

A week later, Scotland overcame Argentina, grinding out a 14-9 success with winger Seam Maitland scoring the only try of the match.

The 2019 Six Nations championship was one of peaks and troughs for a Scotland squad hard hit by injuries. They finished fifth after losing to Wales, Ireland and France and beating Italy before ending with a memorable 38-38 draw with England at Twickenham. They were 31-0 down but mixed some true resolve with stunning flair to grab six tries, and ultimately the lead. It took a last-minute try from England to snatch victory from the Scots' grasp.

The tournament as whole was a below par one for Scotland, but the fightback against England will give them confidence and a positive memory to recollect if things get tough in Japan.

Scotland have four summer test matches as a warm-up to the World Cup; home and away to both France and Georgia.

HEAD COACH

Gregor Townsend is steeped in rugby, especially Scottish rugby. The 46-year-old took over as head coach of Scotland from Vern Cotter in 2017 having enjoyed five successful seasons as head coach of Glasgow Warriors. Townsend was a popular choice, having previously been part of the national coaching set-up from 2008-11, and with a stellar playing career behind him whether at fly-half, centre or fullback. Townsend played 82 times for Scotland, twice for the British Lions, while performing at the highest level for club teams in Scotland, England, Australia, France and South Africa.

He has made Scotland a more dynamic and entertaining team to watch, bringing to their game a style he showed as a player, and making them more difficult to beat especially at Murrayfield.

Something of a maverick, who admits to taking some of his coaching cues from football, he has brought a positivity to Scotland which was slowly building under his predecessor Cotter. He has a signed a new contract which will keep him with the national team until 2021.

PLAYERS TO WATCH

Greig Laidlaw is the feisty, no-nonsense captain of Scotland who has been playing for the team since 2011 and been skipper, on and off, since 2013. He has captained Scotland more often than any other player and, helped by his place-kicking duties, has bagged around 700 points, scoring on average approximately 10 points per match. Having previously played for Edinburgh and Gloucester, he now lines up for Clermont Auvergne in France in the tough Top 14 League. However, he is not guaranteed a starting place, as was proved in the Six Nations, but his experience and place-kicking still make him an important player.

At his best, he is the beating heart of a rejuvenated Scotland team, which is trying to edge up the world rankings, and he has formed a classy partnership with fly-half **Finn Russell**. Russell is a superstar of the game, balancing intelligent match management with an enviable ability with ball in hand or in defence. Currently earning a large salary as an overseas player with Racing 92 in France, he began his professional career at Glasgow Warriors in 2012 where he remained for six years. He has played more than 40 times for Scotland and is the spark which often ignites the team. He is a naturally gifted player and yet to reach the peak of his game. The 26-year-old's best years are still to come.

If Scotland are to overachieve, and reach the semi-finals, Russell will have to prove his world class status. His desire to constantly throw the ball around and use the width of the pitch is a real strength, but also sometimes a concern when his side need to be playing a more conservative style. His second half performance against England in the 38-38 draw at Twickenham in March was a tactical and intuitive masterclass.

Fullback **Stuart Hogg** has pace and passion and is a pivotal player for Scotland. In-form Hogg, 27, who has just joined Exeter Chiefs in the English Premiership after nine successful seasons with Glasgow Warriors, has been described as Scotland's most potent weapon.

Known as someone who loves to win and is temperamental when situations or decisions go against him, Hogg plays on the edge, exciting spectators from all countries. A distant relation of Northern Ireland and Manchester United football legend George Best, Hogg was called 'a once in a generation talent – one of the best players Scotland has ever produced' by a former coach. However, injury limited him to two appearances at the 2019 Six Nations.

In the forwards, lock **Jonny Gray** is someone who should be wearing the blue of Scotland for years to come. The younger brother of Richie, who has also played for the national team and the British Lions, Gray was under-20 captain before being selected for the senior side in 2013. An accurate and pinpoint tackler, the athletic Gray is also lethal in the lineout and passes the ball better than a tighthead forward should. The 25-year-old has played club rugby for Glasgow Warriors since 2012 and is a key figure in an improved, dynamic Scotland pack which punches above its weight.

Don't overlook: **Huw Jones**, who adds creativity to Scotland's midfield, and **Blair Kingholm**, an exciting fullback with an eye for a try.

TEAM STYLE

Before his team won 26-20 at Murrayfield in November 2018, South Africa head coach Rassie Erasmus described Scotland's style as more Southern than Northern Hemisphere, adding: "They are tactically very good, but are not afraid to attack from anywhere on the field." This a huge compliment to a team which has always been built on a determined pack grinding out results and accurate goal kicking. That is no longer Scotland's first-choice approach.

Under head coach Vern Cotter, and now current boss Gregor Townsend, Scotland have shied away from their traditional kicking game and instead towards something more entertaining and expansive. However, they must play smart and finish the opportunities they create, which can be their undoing.

They do not have the power in the forwards to dominate most senior teams and so must adapt their game accordingly. They don't have the big ball carriers of New Zealand or England, so try to maintain pressure by playing the game in the opposing team's half, pouncing on any defensive errors. They are quick, fluid and exciting at their best, but can be naïve in defence.

EXPECTATIONS

It's difficult to see Scotland progressing past the quarter-finals. They are ranked to finish second in the pool, which will probably set up a last-eight tussle with New Zealand. If they do top Pool A, it will likely lead to a quarter-final with South Africa.

Even getting out of the pool will not be straight forward, as hosts Japan and unpredictable Samoa could cause them concerns.

One thing we can expect from Scotland is entertainment, especially if fly-half Finn Russell is at his quarter-back best.

PREDICTION

The Scots' World Cup story will end in the quarter-finals.

SCOTLAND'S POOL A FIXTURES

Ireland: Sunday, September 22 at International Stadium Yokohama, ko 4.45pm (GMT 7.45am)

Samoa: Monday, September 30 at Kobe Misaki Stadium, ko 7.15pm (10.15am)

Russia: Wednesday, October 9 at Shizuoka Stadium, ko 4.15pm (7.15am)

Japan: Sunday, October 13 at Yokohama international Stadium, ko 7.45pm (10.45am)

JAPAN

FACTS

Nickname: Brave Blossoms
World ranking: 11
Qualification: Automatic (RWC 2019 hosts)
World Cup record: P 28, W 4, D 2, L 22
Biggest World Cup win: 52-8 against Zimbabwe (1991)
Biggest World Cup defeat: 145-17 by New Zealand (1995)
World Cups – 8
Performances: Pool stage – 8

RUGBY WORLD CUP HISTORY

Japan have appeared in all eight Rugby World Cups, creating headlines along the way, as they suffered one of the heaviest defeats in the competition's history, while also recording the greatest shock. They have proven themselves to be one of the strongest Tier 2 teams over the decades, and the flag bearers for rugby in Asia.

The Brave Blossoms' first ever match in a World Cup finals saw them lose narrowly 21-18 to the USA in the inaugural competition in 1987. They followed this up with a hefty 60-7 defeat to England but were far from disgraced in their final pool match against hosts Australia, which they lost 42-23.

The 1991 tournament witnessed Japan's first victory, a 52-8 success over Zimbabwe in which they scored eight tries. It was a high point for an aspiring rugby nation, but it would be another 24 years before they would win again.

Their Rugby World Cup roller-coaster ride continued in 1995 when they slumped to an embarrassing 145-17 defeat to a rampant New Zealand team, conceding 21 tries. It was a result which set back the cause of the game in Japan and left many wondering about the participation of Tier 2 teams in the finals.

The comeback took time, and there were other considerable defeats to Tier 1 teams along the way, notably 91-3 to Australia in 2007 and 83-7 to New Zealand in 2011. But redemption came four years later when they were the surprise team of the tournament in England, winning three matches.

Under the guidance of coaching maestro Eddie Jones, Japan beat South Africa 34–32, sending shock waves around the rugby world, before overcoming Samoa 26-5 and the USA 28-18. A 45-10 loss to Scotland meant they finished the pool stage with the same number of wins as Scotland and South Africa, but unlike the other two, they failed to secure any bonus points.

They finished third in the table and so failed to reach their first quarter-finals, but only by the narrowest of margins.

BUILD-UP TO 2019 RUGBY WORLD CUP

As hosts of the 2019 Rugby World Cup, Japan did not participate in last year's Asia Rugby Championship, a competition they have dominated in the last 50 years. Their primary focus was in the second half of 2018 which saw them play seven matches, winning three times.

Under head coach Jamie Joseph, who took up the reins relinquished by Eddie Jones in 2016, Japan hosted Italy in June in back-to-back test matches, winning the first in Oita 34-17 before narrowly losing a week later in Kobe 25-22. They beat Georgia in Tokyo 28-0 the following week to finish off a pleasing summer and useful preparation for a testing tour of Europe. They warmed up with a 31-28 defeat to a World XV in October and then a 69-31 defeat to New Zealand in November, both on home soil.

Joseph said his side took positives away from the defeat to the All Blacks which would stand them in good stead for the Europe test matches. And so it proved as the Brave Blossoms performed admirably in losing 35-15 to England at Twickenham, a result which would have been closer, but for a failure of discipline in the second half.

However, it gave them a boost ahead of their clash with Russia in Gloucester a week later, a match they won 32-27. It also gave them the bragging rights ahead of the two teams meeting in Pool A in this World Cup on September 20.

As part of their World Cup build-up, Japan are scheduled to compete in the 2019 World Rugby Pacific Nations Cup in July and August alongside Fiji, Tonga, Canada, Samoa and the USA. The Brave Blossoms will host two test matches, against Fiji in Kamaishi and Tonga in Hanazono.

Japan will also face a World Cup warm-up match against South Africa on Friday, September 6, two weeks before the tournament begins.

HEAD COACH

Jamie Joseph was a successful player in New Zealand, with Otago, and for New Zealand, with the All Blacks, with whom he reached a Rugby World Cup final in 1995. He later played for Fukuoka Sanix Blues in Japan, qualifying to represent the national team in 1999, recording nine international appearances to add to the 20 he gained with the All Blacks.

With this history, plus more than a decade of coaching provincial teams in New Zealand and the Japan-based Sunwolves in the Super Rugby competition, the 50-year-old former flanker was well suited to take the Japan national coaching job after the enigmatic Eddie Jones left to join England.

A fluent Japanese speaker, Joseph has said it has taken a lot of hard work, but he believes his squad is improving in depth and quality, and that they can reach the last eight of the tournament.

After beating Russia in November, Joseph praised his side, saying: "We knew the Russians would be waiting for us physically and they didn't disappoint. To come back and win that in the second half is a sign of our development as a team. I'm not sure that's a game we would have won a year ago."

Joseph, assisted by coaches John Plumtree and Ben Herring, has been praised for the way he has tightened Japan's often leaky defence.

PLAYERS TO WATCH

Michael Leitch is the talismanic captain of the Brave Blossoms and, if nothing else, will always be remembered as the man who led Japan in memorably defeating South Africa in the 2015 Rugby World Cup.

But the 30-year-old back row player is not finished yet and, with the World Cup being hosted in his adopted home of Japan, can still add to his reputation as a Japanese rugby legend. Born in New Zealand, Leitch moved to Japan when he was 15-years-old to study and has made his life there, winning almost 60 caps for his country and earning citizenship in Japan in 2013. He remains a considerable player and scored a try, narrowly missing out on a second, in the encouraging 35-15 defeat to England at Twickenham in November 2018.

He will be the driving force behind Japan's desire to reach the quarter-finals.

Fly-half **Yu Tamura** has been a consistent performer for the Brave Blossoms since making his debut in 2012, and currently plays for NEC Rockets in the Top League and for the Sunwolves in Super Rugby.

The 30-year-old, who has more than 50 international caps, performed well for Japan against England in November 2018, as did **Timothy Lafaele** at centre. The Samoan-born 28-year-old is one of at least a dozen players who were born outside Japan but have represented the country in the last three years. Lafaele studied in Japan and has played there for his entire professional career with Coca Cola Red Sparks and Sunwolves. His experience and match awareness will be important to Japan.

Equally important will be **Kazuki Himeno**, a powerful 6ft 2in (1.87m) presence at lock forward who, at 25 years old, has the ability to maintain his intensity for 80 minutes, something that not all Japanese players are able to achieve.

An eye-catching World Cup could see him be the next Japanese player given the chance to prove himself with a European club as **Amanaki Mafi** and **Kensuke Hatakeyama** have done before him.

One player who will not feature for Japan is **Ayumu Goromaru** who shot to fame after scoring 24 points in the stunning World Cup victory over South Africa four years ago. After having honours bestowed on him, and even statues erected, and then becoming the highest paid player in the world, he had unsuccessful stints at Queensland Reds and then Toulon, before returning to Yamaha Jubilo in Japan in 2017. To compound Goromaru's fall from grace, Japan head coach Jamie Joseph has said the fullback is no longer in his plans.

Don't overlook: **Ryohei Yamanaka**, a gifted centre, and **Hendrik Tui**, a New Zealand-born loose forward.

TEAM STYLE

Japan's style is based on agility and skill, rather than power and physicality.

Their backs have fine handling skills, as demonstrated in the 2015 Rugby World Cup, and they try to keep the ball moving wide, staying away from the midfield contact areas as much as possible. Their pack does not carry an offensive threat to senior opponents, but good technique means it is not a push over. They play an attractive, open style which should help them engage with even the traditionally subdued Japanese crowds, while making them one of favourite teams with neutrals.

EXPECTATIONS

The weight of expectation on Japan is more burdensome than ever before. Having won three pool matches four years ago, only narrowly missing out on a quarter-final berth, and having shocked the rugby world by beating powerhouses South Africa, the Brave Blossoms will be judged by those lofty standards.

Certainly the Japanese public and the fickle Japan RFU will be expecting great things and neither will be impressed if, as England did in 2015, they fall flat on their faces at the pool stage. Head coach Jamie Joseph was brought in to build on the work of previous boss Eddie Jones and take Japan to the next level. Failure could, however, abruptly end his tenure at the top.

Japan will expect to beat Russia and Samoa, although this is far from a given against an improving European side and an unpredictable Pacific nation. Overcoming Ireland should be a step too far, which means the clash with Scotland on October 13 could be the decider as to which team finishes second in the pool and heads to the knockout stage.

The true test will be whether Japan have the experienced, battle-hardened players who can raise their game when in the spotlight. It is one thing to nip around the heels of senior teams as an underdog, but it becomes something else entirely when expectations have been raised so high.

PREDICTION
No fairy tale for Japan, finishing third in the pool.

JAPAN'S POOL A FIXTURES
Russia: Friday, September 20 at Tokyo Stadium, ko 7.45pm
(GMT 10.45am)

Ireland: Saturday, September 28 at Shizuoka Stadium, ko 4.15pm
(GMT 7.15am)

Samoa: Saturday, October 5 at City of Toyota Stadium, ko
7.30pm (GMT 10.30am)

Scotland: Sunday, October 13 at Yokohama international
Stadium, ko 7.45pm (GMT 10.45)

RUSSIA

FACTS
Nickname: Bears
World ranking: 20
Qualification: 2017-18 European Championship runners-up
World Cup record: P 4, W 0, D 0, L 4
Biggest World Cup win: Yet to win
Biggest World Cup defeat: 62-12 by Ireland (2011)
World Cups – 1
Performances: Pool stage – 1

RUGBY WORLD CUP HISTORY

Russia do not have a tradition of reaching the World Cup finals, in fact they have only reached the tournament once before when it was hosted by New Zealand in 2011. Before this, the Bears refused to enter or failed to qualify which is not surprising. Russia – playing as the Commonwealth of Independent States before 1992 - did not play its first international until 1974, despite the governing body being formed in the 1930s.

In 1995, they came through the preliminary qualifying process before losing to Romania for the place reserved for an Eastern European team. They were expelled from qualifying in 2003 for playing three ineligible South African-born players (Johan Hendriks, Reiner Volschenck and Werner Pieterse) against Spain.

The Bears finally played in their inaugural tournament in 2011 under head coach Nikolay Nerush, who was assisted by Welshman Kingsley Jones. They impressed by scoring eight tries, three of which came against Australia, but they were nevertheless unable to record a victory. They lost 13-6 to the USA, 53-17 to Italy, 62-12 to Ireland, and 68-22 to the Wallabies. Their 2015 qualifying hopes ended in the regional play-off, which they lost to Uruguay.

Russia replaced Romania, and automatically gained qualification to the 2019 Rugby World Cup finals, after an independent committee decided that Romania – as well as Spain and Belgium – had repeatedly fielded ineligible players in the Rugby Europe Championship.

BUILD-UP TO THE 2019 WORLD CUP

After the controversy of their automatic qualification to the World Cup because of rule infringements by Rugby Europe Championship opponents (see above), Russia played four friendlies in 2018 losing 62-13 to the USA, before bouncing back with an impressive 43-20 win over hosts Canada.

A 47-20 success over Namibia and a narrow 32-27 defeat at home to Canada set up their 2019 Rugby Europe Championship. Their record in the championship was a mixed bag, but encouraging, with victories over Belgium (64-7) and Germany (26-18) offset by well-contested defeats to Spain (16-14), Romania (22-20) and champions Georgia (22-6).

Russia will warm-up for the World Cup with matches against Italy and Georgia in August.

HEAD COACH

Former Newport Gwent Dragons and Ospreys boss Lyn Jones has been open in his assessment of Russia's chances at the World Cup.

Speaking three months after being named head coach in August 2018, he told BBC Sport Wales: "We've landed a hot-spot in the Rugby World Cup by default, so we've got a mountain to climb. My appointment was going to be for the long term, but since we've been handed an opportunity to play in the World Cup, that's an Everest in front of me."

He added: "I went in with my eyes wide open, in Tier 2 nations there's a huge (sporting) political system. But there's a lot of good rugby players in Russia, and it's a sleeping giant."

Jones, 55, is known as a somewhat unconventional coach, but one with a solid track record, having led Ospreys to two Celtic League titles and an Anglo-Welsh Cup victory. He coached Namibian team Welwitschias in the South African Currie Cup campaign in 2017.

As a player, Jones was a solid flanker for Neath, earning five caps for Wales in 1993, before his career was ended abruptly.

PLAYERS TO WATCH

Vasily Artemyev brings much needed overseas experience to his role as captain of Russia, having enhanced his game while studying for seven years in Ireland, and having made 33 appearances in top flight English rugby for Northampton Saints from 2011-13. As the first Russian to play in the Premiership, he made an immediate impact for the Saints, scoring a hat-trick against Saracens on his cup debut against Saracens, and then twice more against Newcastle Falcons in his first league match.

Currently playing at fullback or wing back home with Krasny Yar Krasnoyarsk, the 32-year-old has earned almost 80 caps for Russia but is no stereotypical Moscovite, speaking English with a thick Dublin accent.

Another Moscow-born player with overseas experience is 32-year-old lock **Andrei Ostrikov** who has played for Sale Sharks in the Premiership in England since 2011, having previously been with French clubs Agen and Aurillac.

A hard working, intelligent player, Ostrikov is not shy of standing up for himself or his colleagues in the heat of battle and is a fierce tackler. He is perceived by many as being almost irreplaceable in the current Russia team. He made his international debut in 2008 and performed well in the 2011 Rugby World Cup.

Valery Morozov is 1.90m (6ft 3in) tall and weighs 118kgs (260lb) and has been described as a 'monster prop', something which helped entice Premiership side Sale Sharks to sign him in December 2018. The 25-year-old joins up with fellow Russian Andrei Ostrikov at the AJ Bell Stadium.

Sharks' director of rugby said he had been monitoring Morozov's progress with Russian side Enisei-STM, adding: "He's a big, dynamic scrummaging prop, and front row players with his skill set are few and far between." Expect Morozov to feature heavily in Russian game plans at the World Cup.

Yuri Kushnarev has more than 100 Russia caps to his name and the 34-year-old fly-half shows no sign of exiting the international stage just yet. He has been one of the team's best players for many years and, with more than 700 points to his name, his goal-kicking and cool head will be important if Russia are to make their mark in Japan. He is a quality distributor of the ball to some willing runners in midfield, and Russia will need him to be at his best if they are to break the end of their winless run in the tournament.

Don't overlook: **Taguir Gadzhiev**, a mixed martial arts fan and promising prop, and **Dmitry Gerasimov**, a solid centre.

TEAM STYLE
Russia are not afraid to lock horns with any team, relishing the physicality of the game. Their style is to grind down their

opponents and use big ball carriers to crash through defences. It might not be pretty, but it plays to their strengths and, for a Tier 2 rugby nation, they cannot afford to stray too far from Plan A.

Fitness is an issue. Most of the players are with Russian clubs and find it tough to maintain their attritional style for 80 minutes, something that head coach Lyn Jones has come to accept. He has pledged to make his team fitter and more conditioned for the World Cup, something which will also improve the team's confidence and consistency.

EXPECTATIONS

"We have the hosts on day one, then we play Samoa four days after, and as poor as they are for three years, for the World Cup year they can be very tasty with all their big hitters back. Then there's the small matter of taking on Ireland and the 'Scottish Barbarians', so it's a great challenge. We saw huge performances from Japan and Namibia in the last World Cup, so anything can happen on the day."

Those are the words of Russia head coach Lyn Jones more than a year before the start of the 2019 Rugby World Cup, the words of a man who is aware that this country has only ever reached one tournament and is still searching for its first victory.

Realistically, the Bears will be fighting it out with Samoa to see who finishes fourth and fifth in Pool A. For Russia, success will be winning one match, especially as history and the fixture scheduling is working against them. However, with the pressure on Japan to perform on home soil and, as Jones said, with Samoa being famously unpredictable, Russia have a puncher's chance of winning twice.

Russia are often called one of rugby's sleeping giants, but will they be able to stir from their slumber on the biggest stage of all?

PREDICTION
The Bears will be tamed, finishing bottom of Pool A.

RUSSIA'S POOL A FIXTURES
Japan: Friday, September 20 at Tokyo Stadium, ko 7.45pm (GMT 10.45am)

Samoa: Tuesday, September 24 at Kumagaya Stadium, ko 7.15pm (GMT 10.15am)

Ireland: Thursday, October 3 at Kobe Misaki Stadium, ko 7.30pm (GMT 10.15am)

Scotland: Wednesday, October 9 at Shizuoka Stadium Ecopa, ko 4.15pm (GMT 7.15am)

SAMOA

FACTS
Nickname: Manu Samoa
World ranking: 17
Qualification: Repechage play-off champions
World Cup record: P 25, W 12, D 0, L 13
Biggest World Cup win: 60-13 against Uruguay (2003)
Biggest World Cup defeat: 60-10 by South Africa (2003)
World Cups – 7

Performances: Quarter-finals – 2, quarter-final play-off – 1, pool stage – 4

RUGBY WORLD CUP HISTORY

Samoa, previously known as Western Samoa, have a proud record in reaching and performing in World Cup tournaments. For a nation with a population under 200,000, Samoa have consistently punched above their weight, winning almost half of their tournament matches. After being controversially overlooked for an invitation to the first competition in 1987, although they were secretly on standby after a military coup in Fiji threatened that country's attendance, Samoa have qualified for the seven since.

Their first tournament in 1991 was possibly their most memorable. They reached the quarter-finals after finishing second to Australia in Pool C, shocking Wales 16-13 and Argentina (35-12) along the way. They lost 28-6 to Scotland at Murrayfield in the last eight but had made their mark on the international game. Four years later, they again reached the quarter-finals, after overcoming Italy 42-18 and Argentina 32-26 in the pool, only to lose 42-14 to eventual champions South Africa.

In 1999, they again stunned Wales in the pool stage, scoring five tries in beating them 38-31 on home soil at the Millennium Stadium. Samoa edged home thanks to two tries from former All Black Stephen Bachup, and a final try by the excellent Silao Leaegailesolo who also enjoyed a productive kicking game that day. However, a 32-16 defeat to Argentina meant Samoa did not top the group, instead going through to a quarter-final play-off against Scotland, which they lost 35-20.

The four tournaments since then have seen Samoa fail to come through the pool stages, although in 2011 they performed well, beating Namibia 49-12 and Fiji 27-7 and losing in good contests to Wales 17-10 and South Africa 13-5.

BUILD-UP TO THE 2019 RUGBY WORLD CUP

Little ever appears to run smoothly for Samoa between World Cups and this current four-year cycle is no exception. Off the pitch, the finances at the Samoa Rugby Union – in common with most Pacific nations' governing bodies – have potentially hindered the country's progress.

In November 2017, Samoa's Prime Minister and SRU chairman Tuilaepa Lupesolial Sailele Malielegaoi told the world that the organisation was bankrupt and that the players could not be paid for their upcoming tour to Europe. To ease their burden, England's Rugby Football Union gave them a goodwill gesture of £75,000 and covered their costs in the country during their tour. Financial worries aside, inconsistencies remain on the pitch in the run-up to the World Cup.

Samoa failed to qualify automatically for the World Cup from the Oceania group – from which Fiji and Tonga progressed – only reaching the tournament after beating Germany by an aggregate score of 108-43 in the double-header repechage play-off in July 2018. Despite the positive result, head coach Fuimaono Titimaea Tafua was sacked.

In November 2018, the Pacific Islanders came back to Europe to play test matches on three consecutive Saturdays against non-Tier

1 teams, something which did not please new head coach Steve Jackson. Jackson said: "We don't want to be playing Tier 2 teams, but that's just the reality of the situation we're in at the present."

They narrowly lost the first match 30-29 to the USA in Anoeta Stadium in the Basque region of Spain, and a week later they went down 27-19 to Georgia in Tblisi despite leading 19-10 at half-time. They ended the tour on a positive note overcoming Spain 28-10 in Madrid, with two tries coming from Jack Lam, while Rey Lee-Lo and Ed Fidow also dotted down.

Samoa are scheduled to compete in the 2019 World Rugby Pacific Nations Cup in July and August alongside Fiji, Tonga, Canada, Japan and the USA as part of their final preparations for the World Cup.

HEAD COACH

Steve Jackson is a man who speaks his mind and is determined to bring back some pride to a Samoan team lacking confidence and cohesion in recent times. Auckland-born Jackson, 46, has played for New Zealand Maoris, Tasman, Auckland, North Harbour and Southland.

In his first role as head coach, he guided Auckland-based North Harbour to the Championship title, which saw them promoted to the Premiership. He was most recently assistant coach at Auckland Blues.

"I know full well it comes with great responsibility," he said after being confirmed as head coach of Samoa. "We will work hard and are determined to gain the respect of the rugby world." He has since said he wants to create more competition for places by adding depth in key positions in the squad.

On a trip back to Samoa in February 2019, Jackson stressed that lessons had been learned on the Northern Hemisphere tour at the end of 2018, and that he was now fully focused on the World Cup. He said: "The team that comes to the Pacific Nations Cup, hopefully predominantly will be the players that will take the field at Rugby World Cup."

PLAYERS TO WATCH

Chris Vui became the youngest international captain when he took over the role for Samoa in 2016, at the age of 23. Born in New Zealand, the impressive flanker played for North Harbour and then Auckland Blues in the Super Rugby championship, before moving to the English Premiership to represent Worcester Warriors.

On his arrival, Warriors head coach Carl Hogg said: "Chris is a big, powerful and adaptable forward who will certainly add some strength to our pack. At just 23, he is an experienced leader having led North Harbour to the top flight, and we are excited to see what he has to offer." He moved to Bristol Bears in 2017 but continues to impress and is a player and character central to Samoa's hopes of causing a shock in Japan.

Robust and physical are two words often associated with centre **Rey Lee-Lo** and for good reason, packing a power which belies his 1.81m (5ft 11in) and 98kg (216lb) stature. Lee-Lo has played for Hurricanes and Crusaders in Super Rugby and joined Cardiff Blues in Wales in 2015. He is on, what the club called a 'long term deal'.

The 33-year-old says that he has a simple philosophy on rugby. "When I play now, I just treat every game as if it's my last game because you never know what's around the corner in sports these days, especially with injuries and things like that."

Alapati Leiua is an explosive, utility back who plays for Bristol Bears in the English Premiership, having joined the club – now coached by former Samoan star Pat Lam – in 2017 after having played three seasons for London Wasps. Leiua, 30, is described by his club coach as 'consistent,' 'dynamic' and a 'positive influence'– attributes he has brought to the Samoa national team since his debut in 2013.

According to Leiua, New Zealand were keen for him to play for them, but he chose Samoa, the country of his birth, in order to play alongside **Ofisa Treviranus**, his brother who had moved to Europe.

Ahsee Tuala scored two tries, and 22 points in total, when Samoa beat Germany 42-28 in the second leg of the regional play-off to secure a place at the Rugby World Cup. The livewire fullback and finisher has played more than 80 times for Northampton Saints in the English Premiership since 2014, the same year he made his debut for the country in which he was born. He was however, raised in New Zealand from the age of two. Tuala enhanced his reputation as a match-winner when he produced an excellent finish and scored a late try, as 14-man Saints secured a tense 23-22 victory over Stade Francais in the 2016/17 European Rugby Champions Cup play-off final.

Don't overlook: **Jack Lam**, a workaholic in the back row, and Newcastle prop **Logovi'i Mulipola**.

TEAM STYLE

Samoa play a power-based style with their big, mobile ball carriers gaining ground and driving the team forward, while tackling ferociously in defence. They pride themselves on being big-hitters and it is this quality, if sustained for 80 minutes, that can unnerve and damage even the most senior and experienced of opponents.

Off of the pitch, most Samoan rugby players are known as jokers, enjoying their lives and their rugby. But once they cross the white line, they also invoke fear into the hearts of any team that cannot withstand the physical and psychological challenge. With ball in hand, they have options, as their big bruisers can seamlessly evolve into genuine athletes, sidestepping and shimmying their way around static defences.

A relative lack of height throughout the squad makes them susceptible to contestable kicks in open play and at restarts; however, they ultimately remain a threat to any team that they face.

EXPECTATIONS

When Samoa have hit their straps and played with targeted pace and power, they have always shown just how difficult they are to deal with. Just ask any past Wales player. But they have lost their mojo in the last few years, which is evident in their level of confidence on the pitch. By the end of 2018, they had won just 5 of 20 test matches in the previous three seasons, including a double-header victory over minnows Germany in order to qualify for the Rugby World Cup.

Expectations of Samoa replicating their successes during the tournaments of 1991 and 1999 have never been lower. But there is always the hope that under new head coach Steve Jackson, the Pacific Islanders can begin a new era on a positive note.

They have a reputation for saving their best performances for the World Cup, and they also have the pedigree to cause a one-off shock result, which could throw the entire pool into turmoil.

PREDICTION
Fourth place in the pool for inconsistent Samoa.

SAMOA'S POOL A FIXTURES
Russia: Tuesday, September 24 at Kumagaya Stadium, ko 7.15pm (GMT 10.15am)

Scotland: Monday, September 30 at Kobe Misaki Stadium, ko 7.15pm (GMT 10.15am)

Japan: Saturday, October 5 at City of Toyota Stadium, ko 7.30pm (10.30am)

Ireland: Saturday, October 12 at Fukuoka Hakatanomori Stadium, ko 7.45pm (GMT 10.45am)

POOL B

NEW ZEALAND

FACTS

Nickname: All Blacks
World ranking: 1
Qualification: Automatic (Pool C winners in RWC 2015)
World Cup record: P 50, W 44, D 0, L 6
Biggest World Cup win: 145-17 against Japan (1995)
Biggest World Cup defeat: 43-31 by France (1999) & 22-10 by Australia (2003)
World Cups – 8
Performances: Winners – 3; runners-up – 1; third place – 2; semi-finals – 1; quarter-finals – 1

RUGBY WORLD CUP HISTORY

The history of New Zealand at the Rugby World Cup is one of unparalleled success, in comparison to any other nation.

They have competed in all eight tournaments, reaching the final four times and winning three of them. They have won every pool game that they have played and are the only team to have always topped their pool. The All Blacks have scored more points and more tries than any other nation.

It is always a shock when they lose in the tournament, because they begin every match as firm favourites. They have lost just 6 of their 50 matches, and never by more than 12 points. Their worst performing tournament was in 2007 when, after having easily won their pool by scoring 309 points and conceding just 35 in four matches, they lost 20-18 in the quarter-final after a memorable rally by France.

No other team comes close to matching the consistency of the All Blacks. Yet by their own impeccable standards, the country, which has been the No.1 ranked team in the world for virtually three decades, has only recently lived up to expectations in the tournament.

After lifting the Webb Ellis Cup in the inaugural competition, which they co-hosted with Australia in 1987, the All Blacks had to wait 24 years until repeating the feat on home soil in 2011, under legendary head coach Graham Henry.

Led by head coach Steve Hanson, they were world champions again four years later in England where they were rarely challenged. By becoming the first nation to retain the trophy, the All Blacks team became the greatest ever to play the game.

The closest they came to losing was in a bruising semi-final against South Africa at Twickenham, which they eventually edged 20-18. Fly-half Dan Carter then scored 19 points as the All Blacks beat old adversaries Australia 34-17 in the final.

BUILD-UP TO 2019 RUGBY WORLD CUP

Like always, the All Blacks reach the build-up to the Rugby World Cup in form and with a daunting squad of players. Since winning the World Cup four years ago, New Zealand played 42 test matches to the end of 2018, winning 36, drawing 1 and losing 5.

During this period, they enjoyed their longest winning run of 18 test victories (a Tier 1 joint world record held with England) achieved between 2015 and 2016. This form has ensured their position as the No.1 ranked team in the world, and they are again favourites to lift the Webb Ellis Cup after the final on Saturday, November 2 at the International Stadium Yokohama.

However, their air of invincibility has recently been called into question. In a seven-match spell at the end of 2018, they lost twice – 36-34 to South Africa in Wellington and 16-9 to Ireland in Dublin. They also only narrowly overcame South Africa 32-30 in Pretoria and England 16-15 at Twickenham.

Following the defeat to Ireland, All Blacks head coach Steve Hansen said his players were 'gutted' to lose. He added: "This will be very useful, as this team hasn't suffered many [defeats] over the past three years." They bounced back with a 66-3 thrashing of Italy in Rome just a week later.

The All Blacks are scheduled to defend their Southern Hemisphere Rugby Championship crown, albeit in a truncated competition, in July and August just before a World Cup warm-up match at home to Tonga in early September.

If past performances are a guide, the All Blacks will come into the Rugby World Cup bang in form and full of confidence.

HEAD COACH

Steve Hansen had big boots to fill when he took over the role of All Blacks head coach in 2012, but the ones that he will leave for his successor will be even bigger. Being head coach of the All

Blacks is a plum role, but one which has always pushed him into the spotlight. In New Zealand, it is often considered the second highest profile job behind that of the Prime Minister.

All Blacks' success is important, not just for the team, but for a nation of rugby-mad supporters who exhibit a nervous twitch if their heroes are anything other than perfect. If that was not enough, he was replacing the legendary Graham Henry, who retired after guiding the team to success at the 2011 World Cup, during which Hansen was assistant coach.

New Zealand's win percentage has increased to 88 percent in Hansen's tenure, which is three more than when Henry quit, demonstrating just how well he has performed. Hansen enjoyed a modest playing career, performing as a centre for Canterbury 21 times, before later becoming a successful coach with the club, based on the New Zealand South Island.

Hansen replaced Graham Henry as coach of Wales in 2002, taking the principality to the quarter-finals of the 2003 Rugby World Cup, before quitting in 2004 after a turbulent time and returning to New Zealand to act as Henry's assistant at the national side.

World Cup victory in Japan would be New Zealand's third in succession and Hansen's second, having steered them to success in England in 2015 when they dominated the tournament.

Win or lose, he has said he will not coach the All Blacks beyond 2019. "I'd like to coach this team for the rest of my living days, but that's not the right thing to do," he said in December 2018. He added that it was best for the team, which needed 'new eyes' on it, and also for his family with whom he hoped to spend more time.

PLAYERS TO WATCH

When it comes to captains, they don't come much better or more experienced than **Kieran Read,** the current skipper of the All Blacks.

The 33-year-old from Papakura took over the role from the inspirational Richie McCaw in 2016 and has gone on to excel in this high-pressure job, leading from the front. As a No.8 or blindside flanker, Read has scored 25 tries in his 133 All Black appearances, which is more than any other forward currently playing international rugby. He has 43 caps as captain, despite an injury-hit 2017. He was also the IRB Player of the Year in 2013 and a pivotal member of the All Blacks' 2011 and 2015 Rugby World Cup-winning teams.

Assessing Read shortly after taking on the captain's role, All Blacks assistant coach Ian Foster was full of praise. He said: "The biggest accolade I can give him is the way he grew people around him. He has a very inclusive leadership style and encourages a lot of decision-making from the group around him." Read has said that he will retire from international rugby after the World Cup, presumably a decision which will be made easier if he earns a third winners medal.

Someone who is sure to continue playing way past this World Cup is **Beauden Barrett**, the All Blacks fly-half who is considered a genius by many watchers of the game. The 27-year-old was the World Rugby Player of the Year in 2016 and 2017, emulating Kiwi colleague Richie McCaw's record of back-to-back successes, and was nominated in 2018, losing out to Ireland's Johnny Sexton.

He is simply crucial in the All Blacks' attempts to control and dominate the game. For a stand-off, or first five-eighth as they say in the Southern Hemisphere, he is lightening quick which has made him one of the most consistent try scorers for a player in his position, while making him a crucial part of the All Blacks' scrambling defence.

His goal-kicking is usually impressive, but has faltered on the big occasion, notably against the British and Irish Lions in 2017. His recent form is patchy, and he needs an eye-catching World Cup to quiet those who question his claim to the No.10 jersey. His brothers, Jordie and Scott are part of the current squad, while older brother Kane has retired.

Another star Kiwi on the international scene is **Sonny Bill Williams**, although this may not be the case for much longer. Williams, 33, has terrorised defences at centre or on the wing since switching from rugby league to rugby union in 2008. He briefly returned to league and was part of the New Zealand team in the 2013 World Cup, after which he reverted to union again. He is one of few who have played both codes for New Zealand, and he's also played sevens and represented New Zealand in the 2016 Olympics.

Williams has also boxed professionally seven times and never lost. He was a New Zealand and WBA international heavyweight champion until 2013. Injuries have restricted the 34-year-old's game time in recent seasons, and he has hinted at potential retirement after the World Cup.

Ngani Laumape is a centre who is looking to stake his claim for a permanent place in the All Blacks first choice XV. He is seen as a replacement for Sonny Bill Williams and has always impressed after coming off the bench several times.

This World Cup could be the chance for the 25-year-old to shine, having turned down lucrative offers to play in Europe, which would make him unavailable for the All Blacks.

Someone who is timing their form perfectly is **Ardie Savea**, the dynamic open side flanker, who is rated one of the All Blacks' most promising young players. Although initially used as an impact player off the bench, he is now bigger, stronger and fitter than when he first wore the All Black jersey in 2016. Great things are expected.

Don't overlook: **Reiko Ioane**, a 21-year-old winger who could take the rugby world by storm in Japan, and **Brodie Retallick**, who is a world class, all-round lock, almost without equal.

TEAM STYLE

How do you describe the All Blacks' style? They can play any style that they choose on any given day. They aim for Total Rugby; a 100 percent dominance in all areas of the game, something they come closest to than any other team.

Before his team played Italy in Rome in November 2018, head coach Steve Hansen set out how they would play. He said: "Our goal will be to create quality set-piece ball and lightning-quick ruck ball, coupled with real accuracy in our decision making so we can use our skill-sets accordingly." They did and won 66-3.

Just before this, the Sunday Times rugby correspondent Stephen Jones hailed the team's quality. He wrote: "They have torn up the idea that only quick ball, with the opposition on the back foot, is attacking ball. Instead, they have run the ball thrillingly from deep, wide, short; they have run fast ball and slow ball, attacked after their own passes have been dropped."

This is what to expect from the All Blacks in Japan.

EXPECTATIONS

No team has higher expectations among their own players, supporters and neutrals around the world than the All Blacks. Quite simply they will expect and be expected to win every match that they play, clinically and professionally. They are ultimately the team expected to lift the Webb Ellis Cup.

One of the biggest hurdles they will face is the very first Pool B match against world No.5 side South Africa in Yokohama, the winner of which will almost certainly top the pool. The All Blacks have never lost a pool match in the tournament's 32-year history; however, the Springboks were the only team to beat them in the 2018 Rugby Championship and they have beaten them twice in World Cup tournaments.

For an initial match in the World Cup, it is a tough one for both sides. However, even if the All Blacks folded, they should easily cast aside Canada, Namibia and Italy to progress through to the knockout stage.

It would be a huge shock if they did not at least reach the semi-finals, while back at home, anything other than a place in the final would be viewed as a national sporting disaster.

PREDICTION
Red-hot All Blacks to reach the final.

NEW ZEALAND'S POOL B FIXTURES
South Africa: Saturday, September 21 at the International Stadium Yokohama, ko 6.45pm (GMT 9.45am)

Canada: Wednesday, October 2 at Oita Stadium, ko 7.15pm (GMT 10.15am)

Namibia: Sunday, October 6 at the Tokyo Stadium, ko 1.45pm (4.45am)

Italy: Saturday, October 12 at the City of Toyota Stadium, ko 1.45pm (GMT 4.45am)

SOUTH AFRICA

FACTS
Nickname: Springboks
World ranking: 5
Qualification: Automatic (Pool B winners in RWC 2015)
World Cup record: P 36, W 30, D 0, L 6
Biggest World Cup win: 87-0 against Namibia (2011)
Biggest World Cup defeat: 29-9 by New Zealand (2003)

World Cups – 6
Performances: Winners – 2; third place – 2; quarter-finals – 2

RUGBY WORLD CUP HISTORY

South Africa's history at the World Cup is shorter than many Tier 1 nations, having been barred from entering the first two tournaments because of the Apartheid system in their country. However, that makes it more concentrated, having won twice and finished third twice in the six tournaments that they have participated in.

Their most famous moment in the competition came in 1995 when, emerging from the shadows of the sporting embargo, they hosted and famously won the World Cup, beating New Zealand 15-12 in the final after extra-time at Ellis Park in Johannesburg. The image of captain Francois Pienaar being presented with the Webb Ellis Cup by President Nelson Mandela is one of the most iconic moments of the 20th century.

They impressed again in 2007 under captain John Smit when they were champions in France, this time narrowly beating England 15-6 in the final having previously beaten them 36-0 in the pool stage. The Springboks' cause was aided by them avoiding all the senior Tier 1 teams in the tournament, except England.

Third place finishes at the 1999 and 2015 events have underscored the Springboks' consistent record at World Cups and highlighted that they are one of the toughest and most physically demanding teams to face in tournament rugby.

But it's not all positive. Their 34-32 defeat to Japan in the pool stage of the 2015 tournament remains the biggest World Cup shock of all time.

BUILD-UP TO 2019 RUGBY WORLD CUP

It's fair to say that South Africa are in a period of transition and have been since the end of the last World Cup. Allister Coetzee's time as head coach from 2016-18, saw the country slip in the world rankings as low as No.7 and win fewer than half the test matches they played.

Since Rassie Erasmus stepped up from director of rugby to head coach in February 2018, the Springboks won 8 of the 15 matches they played in the following year, recorded a series win over England, and finished second in the Rugby Championship earning a morale-boosting victory over New Zealand along the way.

A shortened Rugby Championship and a warm-up game against Argentina will be the Springboks' last matches to find some sustainable form ahead of the World Cup.

They remain a team with a Rugby World Cup pedigree, but inconsistent recent form. Yet they remain a threat. No team relishes the task of playing against them, and their current unpredictability could work in their favour in one-off tournament contests. Their form and swagger are returning gradually, and they could yet peak at the World Cup.

HEAD COACH

Rassie Erasmus is essentially a stop-gap head coach of the Springboks, holding the chaos at bay just long enough for a punt at the World Cup, before resuming his role as South Africa's director of rugby.

He has, however, stabilised the environment around the team and made them harder to beat. He has also said that he already knows most of the players who will form the core of his World Cup squad.

The 46-year-old is a former coach at Cheetahs, Western Province and Stormers in South Africa. He was also in charge at Munster in Ireland, where he won the 2016-17 Pro12 coach of the year award. With ample Northern and Southern Hemisphere experience, much of which is positive, Erasmus is well placed to mould the South Africa squad and make it one which could challenge at the World Cup.

He will certainly leave nothing to chance, according to Springboks forwards coach Matt Proudfoot who called Erasmus 'dynamic' and a 'master tactician.'

PLAYERS TO WATCH

Siya Kolisi is the first black man to captain the Springboks in their 127-year-history, a role he was handed in 2018.

Many in South Africa saw his appointment as reward for exceptional performances in 2017, and one that can have a cathartic effect on the squad and, more generally, the 'rainbow nation'. Others have wondered whether it was more to do with the country's quota system, which Kolisi himself has said he is not comfortable with at senior level.

The 28-year-old flanker, from the impoverished township of Zwide just outside Port Elizabeth, has represented his country more than 40 times since debuting in 2013. He also starts for the Stormers in the Super Rugby competition. His impact will be act more as an inspiration to the squad and supporters, than as a world class flanker.

Aphiwe Dyantyi is an outstanding young winger who made a name for himself in 2018 by dotting down against England in South Africa's series win, and then scoring two tries in the victory over the All Blacks in Wellington. The 25-year-old now looks like an influential player in the Springboks' back three, just as he has become for Lions in the Super Rugby championship. He was named Breakthrough Player of the Year at the 2018 World Rugby awards evening, further enhancing his growing reputation as a finisher.

Last year was also one to remember for **Malcolm Marx**, a physical and abrasive forward who has been tagged as the best hooker in the world. "The 24-year-old will mix it with the best of them if he has to and, in many ways, symbolises South Africa's desire to return to their former abrasive style of play," said a story on Wales Online at the end of last year.

It continued: "His real threat is at the breakdown, where he is like an extra back-rower pilfering opposition ball and winning penalties regularly. Likely to be one of those spearheading the Springbok World Cup challenge in Japan." That sums him up perfectly.

Scrum-half **Faf de Klerk** is simply one of the best players in the world and, after a sensational 2017-18 season with Sale Sharks in the English Premiership, was shortlisted for World Rugby player of the year. Head coach Rassie Erasmus selected de Klerk for the visit by England during the summer and the Springboks' Northern Hemisphere tour at the end of 2018.

The 27-year-old always stands out because of his shock of blonde hair, but he is also better than most because of his performances last year. Defensively, he is superb, gutsy and fearless. The Springboks are not blessed with depth at No.9, so they will need the combative and technically-improving de Klerk fit and available at the World Cup.

Don't overlook: **Eben Etzebeth**, a fearsome lock who can run through brick walls, and fly-half **Handre Pollard**, whose kicking is crucial to the Springboks.

TEAM STYLE

When rugby fans think of South Africa, they think of a physical team, which often operates in the grey areas of the game's laws. They are gritty warriors who are not shy of pounding their opponents into submission. They maul and scrummage for all that they are worth, and don't take a step back. They have always had, and currently possess, backs with skill and pace. After all, this is the country which produced winger Bryan Habana and scrum-half Joost van der Westhuizen.

However, their brand of rugby has always been built on aggression and bully-boy tactics with less room for creative play than most would like. They like to kick and play the game in the opposition's half. Little has changed over the years, so don't expect anything else at the World Cup.

If the Springboks do find a more open, free-flowing Plan B, when their initial crash-ball tactics falter, they will become even more formidable opponents.

EXPECTATIONS

Let's be honest, few are backing South Africa to win the World Cup in Japan despite their impressive history in the competition, and their ability to be at their best when it comes to tournament time.

However, for these reasons alone they must be considered contenders, plus they are an improving team who, under Rassie Erasmus, beat New Zealand on home soil 12 months ago. Progress and momentum are returning incrementally, and the squad is in a better place than 18 months ago.

Although they have the steel, do they possess the self-belief? The strength in depth of the Springboks' squad is also questionable, especially in the backline. Realistically, they will be expected to finish second behind the All Blacks in Pool B, which would probably pit them against Ireland in the quarter-finals.

A semi-final berth is the best that South Africa can reasonably expect this time around. Anything more would be an over-achievement.

PREDICTION

Springboks' World Cup to end in the quarter-finals.

SOUTH AFRICA'S POOL B FIXTURES

New Zealand: Saturday, September 21 at International Stadium Yokohama, ko 6.45pm (GMT 9.45am)

Namibia: Saturday, September 28 at City of Toyota Stadium, ko 6.45pm (GMT 9.45am)

Italy: Friday, October 4 at Shizuoka Stadium Ecopa, ko 6.45pm (GMT 9.45am)

Canada: Tuesday, October 8 at Kobe Misaki Stadium, ko 7.15pm (GMT 10.15am)

ITALY

FACTS

Nickname: Azzurri
World ranking: 14
Qualification: Automatic (Third place in Pool D in RWC 2015)
World Cup record: P 28, W 11, D 0, L 17
Biggest World Cup win: 53-17 against Russia (2011)
Biggest World Cup defeat: 101-3 by New Zealand (1999)
World Cups – 8
Performances: Pool stage – 8

RUGBY WORLD CUP HISTORY

Italy are an enigma in the rugby world, something which is reflected in their World Cup record. They are officially a Tier 1 nation – one of just 10 in the world – and competed in the Northern Hemisphere Six Nations championship. They have also competed in all eight Rugby World Cups.

However, they have a disappointing world ranking of 14, have struggled to make an impact at the elite level in the last 20 years, and have never reached the World Cup quarter-finals. In seven out of eight tournaments, they have finished third in their pool. Losing two pool matches to the higher ranked teams and winning two pool matches against the lower ranked sides seems to be the World Cup holding pattern in which Italy have found themselves since 2003.

From 1978 to the end of the 2019 Six Nations competition, the Azzurri have recorded 28 victories over Tier 1 nations, perhaps most notably a 20-18 win over South Africa in Florence in 2016. However, none have come in the World Cup.

Italy's first World Cup in 1987, when they were one of the better second tier of nations, saw them score three tries in edging past Fiji 18-15, but also losing 70-6 to New Zealand and 25-16 to Argentina. However, it was a promising start.

Their worst performance came at the 1999 tournament hosted by Wales in which they lost all three of their matches; 67-7 to England, 101-3 to New Zealand and 28-25 to Tonga. Despite this, Italy were ushered in the Tier 1 Five Nations championship, which then became the Six Nations in 2000.

Their best World Cup was arguably in 2011 in New Zealand, when they beat Russia 53-17 and USA 27-10, and played solidly in defeat to Australia (32-6) and Ireland (36-6). Four years ago, they came close to their first World Cup shock when, in a dire match, they ran Ireland close in Pool D, narrowly losing 16-9.

A brilliant performance from Sergio Parisse and three penalties from Tommaso Allan were the highlights, but it was a relative high point in yet another tournament in which the Azzurri failed to hit the headlines.

BUILD-UP TO 2019 RUGBY WORLD CUP

Italy headed into this year's Six Nations championship off the back of a predictably mixed 2018. On a useful tour of Japan in June, playing in Cite and Kobe, they lost the first test match 34-17 before coming back a week later to beat the hosts 25-22. They slumped 54-7 to Ireland in Soldier Field in Chicago, following the high of beating Georgia 28-17. The year ended with defeats to Australia and New Zealand, the latter a 66-3 thrashing.

The 2019 Six Nations proved to be another disappointment for the Azzurri, who have now gone four championships without a single victory. They lost comfortably to England 57-14, although they showed plenty of spirit in going down 33-20 to Scotland, 26-15 to Wales and 26-16 to Ireland. Italy saved their best until last when they dominated large parts of their clash with France in Rome – but were held-up over the try line three times and had a try disallowed - before losing 25-14.

Their World Cup warm-up matches are against Ireland and France in August and England in early September.

HEAD COACH

On taking the reins as head coach of Italy in March 2016, Connor O'Shea said he was 'honoured, humbled and excited' by the challenge, and that Italy as a rugby nation had 'undoubted potential'.

Italian rugby federation president Alfredo Gavazzi said: "O'Shea is a coach with a record of success on the pitch and strong managerial skills, who will add extra value to all of the various components of the Italian rugby set-up."

O'Shea understood the scale of the task; to make the Azzurri more than just a Six Nations and Tier 1 makeweight and guide them to a first World Cup quarter-final. More than two years on, this task remains as elusive as ever.

O'Shea, 48, took on the Italy job after an impressive playing and coaching career. He played for Leinster, London Irish and Ireland, with whom he won 35 caps. O'Shea then moved on to coaching with London Irish in 2001.

Spells followed at the Rugby Football Union as director of regional academies, and the English Institute of Sport as national director with a focus on the London Olympics, before he landed the role of director of rugby at English Premiership side Harlequins.

He spent six mostly successful seasons at The Stoop, finishing when Quins were defeated 26-19 by Montpellier in the final of the European Challenge Cup. Two months later, he was named head coach of Italy, bringing with him as an assistant, former England playmaker Mike Catt.

Up until the end of the 2019 Six Nations championship, O'Shea's Italy had won 6 of their 26 matches under his guidance. But this doesn't bother O'Shea who, in an interview with The Independent in February 2019, said he was focused on laying the groundwork for a stronger game in Italy.

He said: "This is a massive challenge, it's enormous. We know it's about getting the systems right. I'm not bothered about people looking at my stats and results."

PLAYERS TO WATCH

Any assessment of the Italian squad must start with their inspirational captain **Sergio Parisse**. At his best, he is a world class No.8, and has been for many years. He is also admired around the rugby world. He has strength, determination and is mobile with ball in hand, and a tackler of legendary proportions. He has been the last line of defence for a beleaguered Italy rearguard countless times, rallying the troops and then showing them how it's done with bone-crunching tackles.

He can be hot-headed and has had his run-ins with officials, but Parisse, even at the age of 36, is crucial as Italy attempt to break new ground. He has lost more than 100 times as an Italy player, having made a record 140 appearances since 2002. However, this has just made him even more determined.

Tommaso Allan is from a family of rugby players. His Scottish father, William Allan, and his Italian mother, Paola Berlato, both played in Italy where Tommaso was born, while his uncle, John Allan, was capped by Scotland and South Africa.

In a decision that was perceived controversial at the time, despite being eligible to represent Scotland and being courted by them and having even turned out for Scotland Under-20s, he chose to play for Italy at senior level from 2013 onwards.

A skilful fly-half and goal-kicker, with a trademark dummy, he is an all-round playmaker who is comfortable passing, running, or kicking as the situation dictates. At 25 years old, and nearing 50 caps for Italy, he should be wearing the Azzurri's colours for World Cups to come.

Second only to Parisse in seniority, **Leonardo Ghiraldini** was a young star with Italy who grew up to fulfil his potential. The 34-year-old hooker has racked up 10 Six Nations campaigns and three World Cups, he also captained his country, and played for numerous elite level clubs including Leicester Tigers and Toulouse.

He is an awesome scrummager and one of the most experienced hookers in world rugby with more than 100 caps. This will surely be his last crack at a World Cup tournament. Ghiraldini has said he's confident of being fit to play in the World Cup after suffering a serious knee injury against France in the Six Nations in March

Angelo Esposito is at the start of his international rugby journey, which began against Wales in 2014. It's not easy playing on the wing for Italy as your opportunities to run with ball in hand are limited, and your ability to tackle and catch the high ball skills are often tested.

Japan 2019 will be Esposito's first World Cup as a player, and although his opportunities to shine may be few, it is a chance to add to his reputation and secure a long-term back three place.

Don't overlook: **Sebastian Negri**, the brilliant, Zimbabwe-born flanker who plays for Benetton, and fellow flanker **Jake Polledri**, who plays for Gloucester and is a star in the making.

TEAM STYLE

In 2017, Italy bamboozled England by constantly putting a player between scrum-half Danny Care and fly-half George Ford, seemingly in an offside position.

However, by not committing a single player to the tackle area, the referee could not call a ruck, and apart from the tackle area, there is no offside. The Italian players could stand where they wanted, it was perfectly legal, even if morally questionable.

It was a shrewd ploy by Conor O'Shea – which has since been outlawed – foxing the most experienced of England players. The looks of confusion on the faces of England's Dylan Hartley and James Haskell, as they quizzed the referee, were memorable. Italy eventually lost 36-15 but it was 10-5 at half-time and they avoided the feared landslide defeat beforehand. But this inventive game plan is rare from the Azzurri.

They are predominantly a team which is reliant on powerful, courageous forwards, producing a dominant set piece. They can enjoy lengthy periods of possession, and territory is often their friend. However, they lack a cutting edge to turn possession into points. Their frustrating 2019 Six Nations defeat to France highlights this.

They have talent in their backline, among some of the younger players, shown when they scored three eye-catching late tries against Scotland in February. But these came when the game had already been lost.

All of Italy's leaders are forwards, and that says all you need to know about what style to expect from them at the World Cup.

EXPECTATIONS

A total of 32 years of World Cup history, and an inconsistent build-up in the past year, makes it difficult to predict anything other than the usual third place pool finish for the Azzurri.

The positive for them is that they face Tier 2 teams Namibia and Canada at the beginning of the campaign, which should mean that they face the pivotal clash with South Africa off the back of two victories. They will also have had eight days to prepare for the match with the Springboks, the winner of which will probably finish second in the pool behind New Zealand. Pool B is a tough one as New Zealand and South Africa are rugby heavyweights, while Namibia and Canada will be focused on giving Italy good games.

It's more likely that Italy will under-achieve than over-achieve.

PREDICTION

Third place finish in Pool B for Italy, having easily beaten Namibia and Canada and having comfortably lost to New Zealand and South Africa.

ITALY'S POOL B FIXTURES

Namibia: Sunday, September 22 at Hanazono Stadium Higashiosaka, ko 2.15pm (GMT 5.15am)

Canada: Thursday, September 26 at Fukuoka Hakatanomori Stadium, ko 4.15pm (GMT 7.45am)

South Africa: Friday, October 4 at Shizuoka Stadium Ecopa, ko 6.45pm (GMT 9.45am)

New Zealand: Saturday, October 12 at City of Toyota Stadium, ko 1.45pm (GMT 4.45am)

NAMIBIA

FACTS
Nickname: Welwitschias
World ranking: 22
Qualification: Africa Cup champions
World cup record: P 19, W 0, D 0, L 19
Biggest World Cup win: None
Biggest World Cup defeat: 142-0 by Australia (2003)
World Cups – 5
Performances: Pool stage – 5

RUGBY WORLD CUP HISTORY
Namibia's record at World Cup finals is short, but not particularly sweet, having lost all 19 matches they have played.

The country joined the IRB, now World Rugby, in 1991 and within a year the national team had made a remarkable impact on the world stage by beating both Italy and Ireland twice, ending their first full season with 10 wins from 10 contests. Naturally this success rate waned, and they have never been able to produce such form at a World Cup.

The closest Namibia has come to winning was in a Pool C match against Georgia in 2015, which they lost 17-16. Theuns Kotze scored all their points, including a late try, but it was not enough. Their cause was not helped by losing inspirational captain Jacques Burger to injury after 10 minutes.

They have also been on the end of some hefty defeats in their five tournaments, conceding 49 points or more on 13 occasions. They lost their very first tournament match 67-18 to Fiji in 1999, to which 18 other losses have been added, including 142-0 to Australia in 2003, 87-10 to France in 2007 and 87-0 to South Africa in 2011.

Namibia have competed in the last five World Cup tournaments, having qualified by winning the Africa Cup, reaching the 2019 competition after beating Kenya 53-28 in their final regional match in 2017.

The Welwitschias, named after the plant which is the national symbol, dominated the competition scoring more than 50 points in each of their games, including a record 118-0 win over Tunisia.

BUILD-UP TO 2019 RUGBY WORLD CUP

Namibia won the Africa Cup Gold Cup in 2018, for the fifth successive year, to qualify for the Rugby World Cup. The Africa Cup, which took place between mid-June and mid-August, witnessed the Welwitschias beating Uganda 55-6, Tunisia 118-0, Morocco 63-7 and Zimbabwe 58-28 before overcoming their main rivals Kenya 53-28.

Namibia head coach Phil Davies spoke of his pride after the victory over the Simbas in Kampala.

"We played well today, the team stuck to the game plan," he said. "This means a lot, as we have been building a team since the last World Cup. We have an average age of 24 years now compared to 31 at the previous tournament. We have depth now."

Captain Johan Deysel said Namibia beat Kenya because they took the opportunities which came their way. The Welwitschias were back in action at the end of 2018 with a short tour to Europe, which saw them lose 47-20 to Russia, 34-13 to Spain before notching a 29-23 success over Portugal in Taveiro. Tries from Thomasau Forbes, Obert Nortje, JC Greyling and Johann Tromp earned Namibia this morale-boosting win over an improving team which are moving up the world rankings.

Namibia are scheduled to play Uruguay twice in August as part of their preparations for the World Cup.

HEAD COACH

Phil Davies will be aiming to provide Namibia with a more professional build-up to this year's World Cup, certainly in comparison to four years ago.

Former Wales player Davies, 55, had been technical director in Namibia, before being asked to take over the role as head coach when Danie Vermeulen acrimoniously quit the role four months before the start of the 2015 World Cup. Wheelchair-bound Vermeulen cited interference from the Namibian Rugby Union.

Davies guided the Welwitschias to commendable efforts in the tournament and has overseen five Africa Cup titles and a runners-up place in the World Rugby Nations Cup. The former lock, who won 46 caps with Wales, has been coaching for more than 20 years, working with numerous clubs including Cardiff Blues, Worcester Warriors and Llanelli. He currently divides his time between Namibia and Nuneaton of the English Midlands Premier League.

He is known as a master man-manager and has said his role with Namibia is to build an infrastructure, raise standards and upskill local coaches.

Speaking to Wales Online in 2017, Davies explained how Namibian rugby is improving. "We have changed the group a lot. We have got the average age (of the squad) down to about 25 now and have capped something like 21 of our under-20s into senior rugby in the last couple of years," he said. "We have got a national academy, a good daily training environment and we are in the Currie Cup. There is some good stuff going on, it is pleasing, but we are a tier two nation looking to develop so it is always a challenge."

PLAYERS TO WATCH

Renaldo Bothma has been captain of Namibia since the talismanic Jacques Burger retired in 2016. Born in South Africa to a Namibian mother, the 30-year-old has played club rugby for Toyota Verblitz in Japan and for the Bulls in Super Rugby, currently playing as flanker. His greatest strength is his ball-carrying ability, according to Harlequins director of rugby John Kingston, after Bothma signed for the English Premiership team ahead of the 2017/18 campaign.

"Renaldo is one of the most destructive ball carriers in world rugby and so I am absolutely delighted to have secured his services on a long-term contract," he said. "As captain of his country, he also brings strong leadership qualities." These qualities are evident for country as well as club.

He has the world 'SMASH' tattooed on his forearm.

Johan Deysel's most famous moment in the blue of the Welwitschias was the second half try that he scored in the 54-14 defeat to New Zealand in the 2015 World Cup. Despite losing, it was an encouraging performance from Namibia and capped a similarly eye-catching performance from the centre in front of 50,000 at the London Olympic Park.

The 26-year-old, who plays for Colomiers in the French second division and Sharks in the Currie Cup, has also been captain of his country. His experience and ability to finish will be key for Namibia.

Another player with experience and undoubted ability is **Chrysander Botha**, one of the few Namibians who has played club rugby at an elite standard overseas. The former Exeter Chief is a flying, counter-attacking fullback who likes to join the line late, but one who has learned to be comfortable in defence under the high ball after more than 50 international caps.

In an interview with The Rugby Paper, he said of himself: "I can slot in on the wing, but fullback is my preferred position. I'm another attacking threat and if I get the ball early, I can exploit defenders with my pace, use my footwork to create gaps and link and create opportunities for other guys."

Casper Viviers is a hard-working, no-nonsense prop who has been pulling his weight for the Welwitschias since 2010, appearing almost 40 times. Having played in France for seven seasons, Viviers now turns out for the Welwitschias team which competes in the South African domestic Currie Cup. His leadership in the set pieces for Namibia will be important if they are not to be bullied in the pool stage by New Zealand and neighbours South Africa.

Don't overlook: Talented 21-year-old flanker **Prince Gaoseb**, and lineout specialist, lock **Tjiuee Uanivi**.

TEAM STYLE

Asked to describe his team's style, Phil Davies said it is one based on 'courage and flair'. In an interview with RugbyWorldCup.com, shortly after being named head coach, he added: "Obviously we'll work on all the key areas but there will be a big focus on our kicking game, our defence and our turnover attack. Namibian rugby has some great broken field runners…so if we get turnover ball, we can use that to cause the opposition problems on the counter attack."

It will be difficult for Namibia to inflict their style on any of the other teams in Pool B and they are more likely to score through individual brilliance than a tactical game plan. They are mostly a team of amateurs, so are more vulnerable to concede as the match enters the last quarter. However, they will attempt to keep their work rate high, and won't lose because of an absence of determination.

EXPECTATIONS

It isn't about how many matches Namibia can win, but whether they can break their World Cup duck and win at all. And the answer is yes.

Namibia face Canada in their final pool match on October 13, a date which could become historic for the African side. The Canadians have competed in all eight World Cups, but this time needed to triumph in the repechage in order to be the last team to qualify for the tournament.

Assuming New Zealand and South Africa cruise through the pool matches, and Italy do not implode under the pressure of trying to reach the knockout stage, the head-to-head with the Canucks will be the Welwitschias' cup final. It will then be down to which team that can mentally and physically recover from potential drubbings by the three Tier 1 nations.

There is little between the two teams in the world rankings, but it is the one match that the Welwitschias have a realistic chance of winning. If they do, it will be celebrated in the capital, Windhoek, and throughout the country, almost as if they have lifted the Webb Ellis Cup itself. Just as importantly, it will boost the profile of Namibian rugby, as it attempts to restructure and help develop the sport from the grassroots up.

PREDICTION
Namibia will win their first ever World Cup match against Canada to finish the pool in fourth place.

NAMIBIA'S POOL B FIXTURES
Italy: Sunday, September 22 at Hanazono Stadium Higashiosaka, ko 2.15pm (GMT 5.15am)

South Africa: Saturday, September 28 at City of Toyota Stadium, ko 6.45pm (GMT 9.45am)

New Zealand: Sunday, October 6 at Tokyo Stadium, ko 1.45pm (GMT 4.45am)

Canada: Sunday, October 13 at Kamaishi Memorial Stadium, ko 12.15pm (GMT 3.15am)

CANADA

FACTS
Nickname: Canucks
World ranking: 21
Qualification: Regional repechage champions
World Cup record: P 29, W 7, D 2, L 20
Biggest World Cup win: 72-11 against Namibia (1999)
Biggest World Cup defeat: 79-15 by New Zealand (2011)
World Cups – 8
Performances: Quarter-finals – 1; Pool stage – 7

RUGBY WORLD CUP HISTORY
Canada may be a Tier 2 nation – traditionally one of the stronger teams in the Americas (behind Argentina) – yet they have competed in all eight Rugby World Cups, winning almost a quarter of their matches.

They began their World Cup journey in 1987 with a 37-4 victory over Tonga in Napier, New Zealand scoring six tries. They finished third in the pool after losing to Wales and Ireland. Four years later, under the guidance of English head coach Ian Birtwell, Canada put together their most successful tournament by reaching the quarter-finals.

They beat Fiji 13-3 and Romania 19-11 before a narrow 19-13 loss to France which meant they finished second in Pool D, booking a last-eight appearance against world champions New Zealand. Chris Tynan and Alan Charron scored tries in a much-lauded team performance in the 29-13 loss to the All Blacks.

Although Canada have never been able to reach the knockout stages again, they have always been consistent performers and, for a Tier 2 team, rarely been disgraced.

In 1995, they performed well in losing 27-11 to Australia and 20-0 to South Africa after beating Romania 34-3, and then in 1999 fought hard in defeats to France 33-20 and Fiji 38-22 before recording their biggest World Cup victory, 72-11 over Namibia. A 24-7 success against Tonga and a 19-14 defeat to Italy were the highlights of the 2003 tournament, while in 2007 Canada lost three times and drew once (12-12 with Japan). They drew again with Japan (23-23) four years later and repeated their form against Tonga who they overcame 26-20.

The 2015 competition was the Canucks' least impressive as, for the first time, they failed to record a win or a draw. However, they came close, losing 23-18 to Italy and 17-15 to Romania.

BUILD-UP TO 2019 RUGBY WORLD CUP

Canada's route and build-up to the World Cup has been long and hard fought, their place in Japan not being secured until they won the international repechage final on November 23, 2018. They were the last team to qualify.

Having surprisingly failed to qualify via the Americas region automatically or after a play-off with Uruguay, Canada had to play in the four-team repechage final tournament in France, which they won by beating Kenya, Hong Kong and Germany.

Afterwards, head coach Kingsley Jones said the experience of pressure rugby would be beneficial to his team. "It's been a crazy 12 months, I think I've done 50,000 air miles," he said. "Obviously I'd have taken a win over Uruguay because, as a coach, you want to win every game, but it wasn't meant to be. Anyway, I'd already told myself when I took this job that the best pathway for us to be competitive at the World Cup is through the repechage, because it would give us a chance to play three games together as a group of core players, which probably won't happen again until July. It also gave us a chance to win something together and build as a team. I am hoping that it will stand us in good stead going forward."

So far this has not been the case for Canada, whose lack of confidence will not have been helped by losing four of their five Americas Rugby Championship fixtures in 2019, finishing the six-team tournament in fifth place.

With most of their marquee players abroad with professional clubs, Canada began with a morale-sapping 20-17 setback to Uruguay, after which they surprisingly lost to Brazil 18-10, and an Argentina XV 39-23. However, the toughest of all to bear was when they lost 30-25 to the USA. The only success was a 56-0 thrashing of Chile.

Canada are scheduled to compete in the 2019 World Rugby Pacific Nations Cup in July and August alongside Fiji, Tonga, Samoa, Japan and the USA as part of their final preparations for the World Cup.

HEAD COACH

On being named as Canada's head coach in September 2017, Kingsley Jones said: "Our immediate priority is attaining qualification for the Rugby World Cup, this is critical." He did achieve this, although it took more than a year of travelling and intense rugby.

Jones, 50, won 10 caps as a flanker for Wales and has gone on to have a strong coaching career at Sale Shark, Newport Gwent Dragons and Russia. Jones took charge of a Canadian team from Mark Anscombe which was bereft of confidence and form. Their world ranking had been on the slide since 2015, when they enjoyed a solitary victory and suffered a whitewash at that year's World Cup in England.

Since taking the reins, Jones has overseen a painfully slow return to the kind of form expected by Canada and, most importantly, a place at Japan 2019.

PLAYERS TO WATCH

Phil Mack has more than 50 international caps to his name and, as captain and scrum-half, he is vital to the game management and strategic approach of the Canucks. As a former elite sevens player, his ball handling skills and savvy approach at the breakdown are well known.

The 34-year-old has played for the national team since 2009 at the 15s and sevens game and is currently playing his club rugby for Seattle Seawolves in Major League Rugby, the elite level professional rugby tournament in the USA.

Mack is a member of the Vancouver Island Toquaht first nation and helped set up the First Nations Rugby Club. He is a stalwart of the Canadian game and a mentor to many, especially among the country's first nation young sports men and women.

Nick Blevins has been a stalwart of the Canada squad since making his debut in 2009, amassing more than 50 caps and points during his time in the red jersey. The 30-year-old plays for Canadian club team Prairie Wolf Pack and is known as a powerful centre with ball in hand and in defence and will be keen to be part of a team which performs better than at the last World Cup in England.

Ciaran Hearn is another player with plenty of experience of international and overseas club rugby. The 33-year-old versatile back signed for London Irish after the 2015 World Cup and, after an injury-ravaged 2017-18 season, is back to his best for the Premiership team.

He also started well for Canada in the Americas Rugby Championship this year, scoring two tries to add to his useful goal-kicking performances. He has more than 60 international caps to his name.

Lucas Rumball proved his worth as a flanker and captain for Canada at this year's America Rugby Championship. The 24-year-old, who plays for Toronto Arrows, spoke of his approach to the game last year.

"When I go in, I'm giving it my best at whatever it is," he said. "If I'm not doing that, there's really no point in doing it. There's nothing stopping you from enjoying it while you're working hard. There are definitely some crappy times and some hard times, but at the end of the day, you need to really enjoy what you're doing."

Don't overlook: New Zealand-based hooker **Jordan Olsen**, and brilliant fly-half **Daniel van der Merwe**, who is battling to overcome a shoulder injury.

TEAM STYLE

It's not easy to predict what style of rugby Canada will present the world in Japan due to the lack of form and confidence that has dogged them in recent years.

Traditionally, they have had powerful players all over the park and have fronted up well to the physicality of Tier 1 teams, whether from the Northern or Southern Hemisphere. If playmaker and leading try-scorer Daniel van der Merwe has not recovered from his shoulder operation at the start of 2019, then Canada will not be so confident about playing an open game and will probably attempt to grind out victories.

The Canucks will be determined and uncompromising, but it may not be pretty or even effective.

EXPECTATIONS

The pressure on a Tier 2 team such as Canada firstly comes from qualifying for a World Cup. For the first time, the Canucks edged their way into this tournament after coming through the repechage system. Making the finals is worth $10million to Canadian rugby, according to head coach Kingsley Jones, a fortune to the country's governing body. So initially, it's job done.

Now they just have to perform at the finals, not just because they want success, but because a third-place finish in the pool –

which is what success looks like to Canada – will earn them an automatic qualification for the 2023 Rugby World Cup in France. To achieve this, they will need to raise their standards against Namibia and Italy.

"Let's be realistic about it, we've got a chance of winning two games," said Jones. "But we'll have to play our best and have a bit of luck and have everyone in form. As far as I am concerned, our next target is to qualify for 2023, and the best opportunity to do that is in September and October (the World Cup)."

Canada are normally a sound bet to win at least one pool match and for locking horns with senior teams, something they have proved over the last 32 years. But they are currently at a historically low ebb, struggling with the depth of their squad and fragile confidence levels. They may beat Namibia, but that won't be easy, and it would require a considerable change of fortune for them to be able to do any more.

PREDICTION
The Canucks fail to fire and finish winless and bottom of the pool.

CANADA'S POOL B FIXTURES
Italy: Thursday, September 26 at Fukuoka Hakatanomori
Stadium, ko 4.45pm (GMT 7.45am)

New Zealand: Wednesday, October 2 at Oita Stadium, ko 7.15pm
(GMT 10.15am)

South Africa: Tuesday, October 8 at Kobe Misaki Stadium, ko 7.17pm (10.15am)

Namibia: Sunday, October 13 at Kamaishi Memorial Stadium, ko 12.15pm (3.15am)

POOL C

ENGLAND

FACTS

Nickname: None

World ranking: 4

Qualification: Automatic (third place in Pool A in RWC 2015)

World Cup Record: P 44, W 31, D 0, L 13

Biggest World Cup win: 111-13 against Uruguay (2003)

Biggest World Cup defeat: 36-0 by South Africa (2007)

World Cups – 8

Performances: Winners – 1; runners-up – 2; fourth place – 1; quarter-finals – 3; pool stage – 1

RUGBY WORLD CUP HISTORY

England have competed in all eight tournaments and are the most successful Northern Hemisphere team in Rugby World Cup history, having lifted the Webb Ellis Cup in 2003 and finished runners-up on two other occasions.

They are one of the most consistent performers at World Cup finals and have always reached the knockout stages until the humbling 2015 tournament, which they hosted. Having eased past Fiji 35-11, they were then beaten 28-25 by Wales after conceding a Gareth Davies try – converted by Dan Biggar – with 10 minutes remaining, ultimately levelling the score. A penalty by Biggar on 75 minutes proved to be the difference between the teams.

England followed this up with a 33-13 defeat to Australia, and although they finished with a 60-3 success over Uruguay, they crashed out of the tournament at the pool stage for the first time. If this is the low point of England's World Cup story, and of that there is no doubt, their dramatic victory in 2003 was undoubtedly their crowning glory.

Heading into the tournament as the world's No.1 team and favourites, Clive Woodward's side eased into the final after winning Pool A, and then overcoming Wales 28-17 in the quarters, and France 24-7 in the semis. The final proved a memorable one against hosts Australia, who had defied the odds in going so far in the competition. The match was decided by a last-gasp drop goal from player of the tournament Jonny Wilkinson, England dramatically edging it 20-17.

England have also reached the final on two other occasions, losing 12-6 to Australia at Twickenham in 1991 and 15-6 to South Africa at the Stade de France in 2007.

BUILD-UP TO 2019 RUGBY WORLD CUP

Since Eddie Jones became head coach in 2015, England have been on something of a roller-coaster ride when it comes to form, having produced extended periods of both success and failure. They equalled the world record number of 18 consecutive victories set by New Zealand, before their run ended when they lost the last game of the 2017 Six Nations to Ireland 13-9.

Since February 2017, their form has been more inconsistent. 2018 was a particularly tough year for England who initially lost five matches in succession to Scotland, France, Ireland and South

Africa (twice). As if to highlight that their highs and lows come in waves, England finished off the year by winning four of their five matches, their only loss being a 16-15 nail-biter with New Zealand at Twickenham.

The 2019 Six Nations initially promised so much but ended with frustration and more questions than answers. Eddie Jones' England ultimately finished as runners-up to champions Wales, who overcame England 21-13 en route to winning the Grand Slam. England opened the championships in eye-catching form beating Ireland 32-20, and following up with impressive successes over France (44-8) and Italy (57-14). They finished in worrying fashion, failing to build on a 31-7 half-time lead against Scotland and needing a late try to draw 38-38.

England have scheduled World Cup warm-up matches against Wales, Ireland and Italy in August and early September.

HEAD COACH

When England replaced Stuart Lancaster with Eddie Jones, they were replacing an Englishman with an Australian, a pragmatist with a maverick, a conciliator with a street fighter. They did this soon after the end of the disastrous 2015 Rugby World Cup, which they hosted but exited at the pool stage. It is difficult to pigeon-hole Jones the man and the coach, as he divides opinion like no other.

Jones, 59, is married to a Japanese woman, and was born in Tasmania to a Japanese-American mother and an Australian father. He played rugby to provincial standards in Australia and after a brief career in teaching, he took over as coach of Randwick in 1994. Club coaching in Australia and Japan followed, and then in 2001, he was named Australia head coach. He led the Wallabies to the 2003 World Cup final, which they narrowly lost to England. He was also an assistant coach to South Africa when they won the World Cup in 2007. He coached Saracens in the English Premiership for two seasons before taking the reins of Japan, guiding them in the 2015 World Cup and to a famous underdog victory over South Africa.

His strengths are talent identification and a willingness to take chances on players that he considers exciting and dangerous. His selection policy is rarely conservative, and he works hard with individual players, providing them with plenty of support and clarity. He is also comfortable rattling a few cages and playing mind games, whether it is within the set-up or through the media about opposition teams and coaches.

On being named England boss he said: "The opportunity to take the reins in possibly the world's most high-profile international rugby job doesn't come along every day, and I feel fortunate to be given the opportunity."

He has driven his team to win two Six Nations titles and equalled the world record for consecutive victories but has also presided over fallow periods. His task of making England World Cup champions again, and a consistent performer at the top table of international rugby, is still a work in progress. But he has made the team more watchable, inventive and creative, and certainly more unpredictable.

Jones' contract with England expires in 2021, although there is a break clause if they under-perform in Japan.

PLAYERS TO WATCH

Owen Farrell has recently taken on the mantle of captain and is the lynchpin at fly-half around which England's performances so often depend but can also falter. Farrell comes from a family with rugby running through its veins.

His father Andy and grandfather are former professional rugby league players, which Owen initially played at junior level, while his cousin Liam Farrell and uncle Sean O'Loughlin are still in the game with Wigan.

He began playing rugby union when his father, a forwards coach with Ireland and their next head coach after the World Cup, switched codes to play for Saracens where Owen now performs. He was the youngest player in English professional rugby when he played for Saracens just 11 days after his 17th birthday.

The 28-year-old has outstanding skills and a big match temperament, which has seen him nominated on the shortlist for the World Rugby player of the year award. His goal kicking is metronomic, and he is a composed playmaker, but not necessarily the most instinctively creative No.10 in world rugby.

Billy Vunipola is at the heart of England's planning for the World Cup, if they can keep the Saracens No.8 fit for any length of time.

Australian-born to Tongan parents, who qualified to play for England under residency rules, 26-year-old Vunipola is in his prime, bringing raw power and dynamism to the back row and to England's impressive blitz defence.

Described as a 'rugby bulldozer', England have struggled during his many absences caused by injuries including a broken arm. They are desperate to keep him fit for Japan. Vunipola was given a formal warning in April by the RFU, rugby's governing body in England, for 'liking' a homophobic Instagram post from Australian player Israel Folau.

His brother **Mako Vunipola** plays prop for Saracens and is also part of the England squad.

Jonny May can divide opinion in the rugby world, but there is no denying his electrifying pace and coveted finishing skills.

When he is in form, as he has been for the past 18 months, the Leicester Tigers winger is a fans' favourite with his weaving runs from deep or laser-guided chasing of the high ball. The 30-year-old is enjoying an extended run in the England team, scoring 12 tries in as many tests at one stage, and closing in on 50 international appearances.

Tigers teammate Ben Youngs called him the best winger in the world after he scored a hat-trick of tries as England beat France in the Six Nations.

In an interview with Sky Sports in February 2019, May said his new-found consistency is down to experience. "I have scored a lot in my last 12 months – more than in my first 30 games – is that luck or coincidence? Maybe it is, but I know my game is better now and the tries come with that."

Closer to the engine room of the team, **Tom Curry** may only be 21 years old but he more than holds his own in a formidable

England back row and is quickly becoming a match winner for his country. The Sale Sharks flanker was capped when only 18, such was his obvious talents and maturity according to Eddie Jones.

Curry, whose twin brother Ben also plays for Sale, has energy and industry which complements some of the big ball carriers around him, and his tackle count in a match is rarely beaten. He is set to be a mainstay of the England team for World Cups to come, and Japan 2019 could be just the platform to formally announce himself to the rest of the world.

Don't overlook: **Kyle Sinckler**, a hard tackling if temperamental prop, and **Manu Tuilagi**, a man-mountain in England's midfield with or without the ball.

TEAM STYLE

As should be expected from a team coached by Eddie Jones, England's style is constantly evolving. Although England were traditionally more comfortable with a conservative approach based on an organised pack, brutal defence and accurate kicking, they now possess the strength to move the ball wide to a lightening quick back and use powerful runners to smash through midfield or revert back to type as required.

In this year's Six Nations championship, in which they finished second, England often used a blitz defence to close down their opponents, a physically demanding tactic to maintain for 80 minutes. When they had the ball, England used their heavyweight midfield and back row to make ground, suck in defenders and then kick to the corners.

Playing the game in the opposition's half is always a good idea and they have recently taken this approach to the extreme – drummed into them by assistant coach John Mitchell – and have been successful. However, when playing against Wales in February, England's game plan was poorly executed, and they showed a lack of judgement or instinct when a change to an alternative option was required.

In their final 2019 Six Nations clash against Scotland in March, England displayed the best and worst of their traits. England ran away with the first half 31-7, playing with an irresistible mixture of pace, power and individual brilliance. They were ponderous and static in the second period and were fortunate to score a late try to draw 38-38.

Their go-to game plan will overpower most teams, but when this falters, their ability to play heads-up rugby is questionable. They have become a team which begins well, scoring early points and initially dominating, but their habit of falling away in the second half is becoming a feature.

They will have worked on a suitable Plan B by the time the World Cup comes around and it could involve giving the ball more often to the new kid on the block Joe Cokanasiga, a mobile skyscraper on the wing who carries the ball in one hand and poses a Jonah Lomu-style threat.

EXPECTATIONS

England have the squad strength, the playing and coaching experience, and the recent form to be one of the contenders to lift the Webb Ellis Cup. However, one of their greatest hurdles is being drawn in probably the toughest pool in the competition.

While France, Argentina, the USA and Tonga are all outside the top seven in the world rankings, and England are ranked No.4, none of these teams are cannon fodder – not even close. France and Argentina are Tier 1 teams who are consistent performers in the World Cup, while the USA and Tonga are physically strong teams looking to prey on any apprehensions shown by their senior opponents.

England will be expected to win the pool with France trailing in second place, but it's easy to see Argentina potentially bringing down one of the favourites. Bonus points could be crucial in this pool.

If they are not too worn down by the granite-tough nature of their pool matches, England should be well set for a quarter-final, probably against Australia. The semi-final is the minimum expectation from England who, given Eddie Jones' knowledge of Japan, will be well prepared for the various conditions and stadiums they will face.

England could also find strong support from Japanese fans looking for a second team to cheer.

PREDICTION

England should reach the semi-finals but their propensity to crumble at key moments might prevent them going all the way.

ENGLAND'S POOL C FIXTURES

Tonga: Sunday, September 22 at Sapporo Dome, ko 7.15pm
(GMT 10.15am)

USA: Thursday, September 26 at Kobe Misaki Stadium, ko
7.45pm (GMT 10.45am)

Argentina: Saturday, October 5 at Tokyo Stadium, ko 5pm (GMT
8.00am)

France: Saturday, October 12 at International Stadium
Yokohama, ko 5.15pm (GMT 8.15am)

FRANCE

FACTS

Nickname: Les Bleus
World ranking: 8
Qualification: Automatic (runners-up in Pool D in RWC 2015)
World Cup record: P 48, W 33, D 1, L 14
Biggest World Cup win: 87-19 against Namibia (2007)
Biggest World Cup defeat: 62-13 by New Zealand (2015)
World Cups – 8
Performances: Runners-up – 3; third place – 1; fourth place – 2;
quarter-finals – 2

RUGBY WORLD CUP HISTORY

For all their famous inconsistency, France have an impressively
consistent record at World Cup finals, although they are yet to be
champions.

They have appeared in all eight World Cups and have always progressed through to the knockout stage. They have reached the final on three occasions, coming closest in 2011 under Marc Lievremont despite a falling out between the head coach and his players.

Having finished second in their pool, although almost being tripped up by Tonga before winning 19-14, France edged out England 19-12 in the quarter-final and Wales 9-8 in the semi-final before losing a dramatic final 8-7 to hosts New Zealand.

France were at their best in this final and had New Zealand reeling at times but could only manage a Thierry Dusautoir try early in the second half converted by Francois Trinh-Duc. It was payback for the All Blacks who had seen their tournaments in 1999 and 2007 ended by comeback victories by Les Bleus. France won a place in the final of the inaugural tournament in 1987, losing 29-9 to New Zealand, and were also beaten in the 1999 final, going down 35-12 to Australia.

Having also finished third once and fourth twice, France have reached at least the semi-finals in six of their eight tournaments. Their least successful tournament was in 2015 when they lost 24-9 to Ireland in the pool match at Cardiff's Millennium Stadium, and then suffered their heaviest ever tournament defeat when they were thumped 62-13 by the All Blacks in the quarter-final at the same venue.

BUILD-UP TO THE 2019 RUGBY WORLD CUP

A team's form in the 12 months leading to a World Cup is often vital to their chances of success, but this rule does not really apply to Les Bleus. If history is to be believed, the form guide can be cast aside as it bears little relationship to how France perform in the competition, such are their eccentricities and Gallic mood swings.

Under Jacques Brunel, who took over the thankless role of head coach in December 2017 from Guy Noves, France have continued to struggle to put back-to-back victories together, losing 11 of his first 16 matches up to the end of the 2019 Six Nations. That championship offered France little in the way of hope going forward as, even for the French, they were incredibly disorganised and bordering on shambolic.

They lost 24-19 to Wales before being thumped 44-8 by England, their biggest defeat to their old rivals and generally in the Six Nations since 1911. Then followed a 27-10 success over Scotland and a 26-14 defeat to Ireland before riding their luck to beat Italy 25-14.

France are scheduled to play Scotland twice and Italy in World Cup warm-up contests in August.

HEAD COACH

When Jacques Brunel was appointed France head coach, he said he wanted to simplify the way that the team played but warned 'it's complicated to make things simple'.

The former Perpignan and Bordeaux Begles coach insisted his emphasis with the team would be on speed, intensity and restoring confidence after just 7 wins in 21 matches during Noves' reign.

He has yet to achieve these aims and in many ways has fanned the flames of more internal dissent and acrimony.

He was known as a strong man-manager, and one who could cajole and inspire players to pull in the same direction, something which is not always the case with a French team. But there are issues with having too little time with players because of the length of the domestic season and a general drop in the technical ability of French players in the last decade.

Brunel, 65, coached Italy from 2012-16 and was France assistant coach from 2001-07 during which time they won the Six Nations on four occasions and completed the Grand Slam in 2004. However, his current record with France is worryingly similar to his predecessor and, if the players' often exasperated looks to the bench during the Six Nations are a reliable indicator, his management skills are now being questioned.

He has used more than 60 players in under 18 months and failed to unite the disparate talents of Ntamack, Ramos, Demba Bamba and others.

PLAYERS TO WATCH

Guilhem Guirado became captain of France in 2015, and the Toulon hooker, who is joining Montpelier next season, is a mainstay of the team, combining expert scrummaging skills with leading a fractured group of players.

Ahead of the 2019 Six Nations, he said: "We have struggled to build the team spirit we need. It has proven very difficult. The players are playing well at their clubs, but the problem is the transition back to international rugby."

Guirado, 33, is a strong character and will need to be in order to energise a scrum, which was once feared, but in recent times has become tame by comparison.

Louis Picamoles is a hugely experienced back row or No.8 whose pace, power and size make him an awkward opponent to put down.

Good handling skills and the ability to offload make him an important weapon in the French arsenal, yet for someone who has been playing international rugby for more than 10 years and has an excess of 70 caps, he has not always warranted a regular starting place. The Montpellier player has hinted that he may retire from international rugby after Japan 2019 so will be focused on finishing a memorable career on a high.

Morgan Parra's nickname in the French team is Little General, highlighting his vocal marshalling qualities at scrum-half. He is a favourite with supporters and has been for most of the 10 years he has played international rugby, a period which has seen him rack up more than 70 caps.

The 30-year-old, of Portuguese extraction, is also a reliable place kicker, something that France miss when he is not in the team, although his accuracy has waned since a recent hip injury. However, he remains an experienced influencer within the squad and someone who is capable of unlocking that elusive Gallic flair.

Someone just beginning their international story is **Damian Penaud**, a fast, silky runner at centre or wing. The 22-year-old plays for Clermont and is the son of former French international Alain Penaud.

He has produced some eye-catching performances for his club and brought that form to the international scene, which is not easy in a period when the French team is struggling. There is no denying his skills with the ball, but his defensive game is still unproven and needs work if he is to perform on the biggest stage.

Don't overlook: **Thomas Ramos**, a free-running fullback who made an impressive international debut in February, and **Wenceslas Lauret**, a solid flanker (or lock) who rarely puts a foot wrong.

TEAM STYLE

To France's credit, they have the ability in their squad to play various styles, and often do in a single match, whether they plan to or not.

Recent struggles have dented their all-important confidence, an attribute France need if they are to reproduce the rugby for which they are rightly remembered, and of which they are proud. France have adopted a more conservative approach of late – brawn over inventiveness – but it has not greatly improved the squad's mood or results.

They have also introduced players who have shined in their successful under-20s team of recent years – like Penaud, Ramos,

Antoine Dupont and Romain Ntamack – and while that is promising, it has yet to pay dividends. There are also question marks over their kicking and fitness.

They showed in the 2019 Six Nations that they are at their best when playing heads-up rugby, offloading and counter-attacking with *jour de vivre*. Their efforts in the first half against Wales were exciting and a joy to watch, leading them to a 16-0 half-time lead. But Les Bleus' second half performance was disorganised and without focus, and they ultimately lost the match 24-19.

From the outside looking in, it's unclear what style France will adopt to give themselves the best chance of success at the World Cup and, until the first match kicks off, the team probably won't know either.

EXPECTATIONS

This is a team which has a history of defying the odds and, regardless of form or a discernible game plan, have an impressive record at World Cup tournaments. So, it is not unreasonable to once again expect them to overcome their flaws and self-inflicted wounds and deliver a respectable tournament, perhaps a semi-final place.

But this time the chaos surrounding Les Bleus seems more genuine, the weaknesses more technical, the talent pool shallower and the brilliance more fleeting, lacking in lustre. France were poor in the 2015 tournament but did reach the knockout stages. This time around their first match is against Argentina, and the Pumas will be sniffing blood, as overcoming France will be their best shot of progressing out of the pool stage.

France could once again surprise, but if they lose to Argentina, their World Cup could be over before it has even started.

PREDICTION
They will probably reach the quarter-finals, but if Les Bleus are off-colour they could fail to exit the pool stage for the first time.

FRANCE'S POOL C FIXTURES
Argentina: Saturday, September 21 at Tokyo Stadium, ko 4.15pm (GMT 7.15am)

USA: Wednesday, October 2 at Fukuoka Hakatanomori Stadium, ko 4.45pm (7.45am)

Tonga: Sunday, October 6 at Kumamoto Stadium, ko 4.45pm (7.45am)

England: Saturday, October 12 at International Stadium Yokohama, ko 5.15pm (8.15am)

ARGENTINA

FACTS
Nickname: Los Pumas
World ranking: 10
Qualification: Automatic (runners-up in Pool C in RWC 2015)
World Cup record: P 37, W 19, D 0, L 18
Biggest World Cup win: 67-14 against Namibia (2003)
Biggest World Cup defeat: 46-15 by New Zealand (1987)

World Cups – 8
Performances: Third place – 1; fourth place – 1; quarter-finals – 2;
pool stage – 4

RUGBY WORLD CUP HISTORY

Argentina are flagbearers for Americas rugby and particularly at the World Cup where they have increasingly become a team of which to be wary. The Pumas have attended all eight tournaments, really hitting their stride at the last three - finishing third in 2007, fourth in 2015 while reaching the quarter-finals in 2011, something they also did for the first time in 1999. Their rise from a Tier 2 nation to a Tier 1 nation has been reflected in the improving set of results they have strung together at World Cups.

The 2007 competition in France was their high-water mark after beating the hosts in the opening match 17-12, and then Ireland 30-15 to top a strong Pool D – the only time they have achieved this feat. This was followed by a 19-13 success over Scotland in the quarter-finals before they succumbed to eventual champions South Africa 37-13 in the semis. Argentina, coached by Marcelo Loffreda, capped a memorable tournament by overcoming France for a second time, the 34-10 score line earning them the bronze medal.

In 2011, they reached the quarter-finals after finishing second in Pool B, a group they would have won if it wasn't for their narrow 13-9 defeat by a rattled England team. Under the guidance of head coach Daniel Hourcade, the Pumas also impressed in 2015 in England. They began with a hard fought 26-16 setback to New Zealand in the first Pool C clash, to which they responded by scoring an impressive 163 points in total against Georgia, Tonga, and Namibia.

An outstanding team performance, in which Jose Imhoff scored two of their four tries, earned them a 43-20 victory over Ireland in the quarter-finals before losing to Australia in the semi-finals (29-15), and to South Africa in the bronze medal match (24-13).

BUILD-UP TO THE 2019 RUGBY WORLD CUP

The Pumas endured a tough 2018 in which they won just 2 of their 13 matches; 32-19 at home to South Africa in August and 23-19 away to Australia the following month.

However, both were in the Rugby Championship – formerly the Tri-Nations – with the victory over the Wallabies being particularly noteworthy, as it was the first time they had won in Australia since 1983. A long-range penalty from Emiliano Boffelli with three minutes remaining sealed a fine win, and although they finished the championship in last place, their record of two wins was shared by Australia.

They were also leading the return leg against the Wallabies by 24 points before eventually losing 45-34. Defeats to Ireland, France, Scotland and the Barbarians at the end of the year were disappointing, but not surprising according to new head coach Mario Ledesma.

"The goal of our tour was to breed a couple of new players and try new combinations and keep learning," he said. "We only started with the team four months ago and we are all learning – staff and players." Hooker Julian Montoya summed up the mood by saying it had been a 'tough, tough tour'. So, the Pumas' form is indifferent, but improving under Ledesma.

They do not have many test matches in which to overturn this form in the build-up to Japan, but they will feel that they are in a better place than they were 12 months ago.

In July and August, Argentina are scheduled to face New Zealand, Australia and South Africa in the truncated Rugby Championship, and then South Africa again, and a French Barbarians XV in the run-in to the World Cup.

HEAD COACH

"We must work in defining our identity and setting up structures, but it is very clear that all of what we do from now on will be useful in preparing for Japan next year."

This is what Mario Ledesma said after being appointed as Argentina head coach in August 2018, six weeks after the resignation of Daniel Hourcade who presided over 15 defeats in his last 17 matches. Ledesma also spoke about how this was his dream job, but for the Argentine Rugby Union, this was also a dream appointment.

The 46-year-old former hooker was capped 84 times by the Pumas in a 15-year career and played in four World Cup tournaments. His short coaching journey has been equally impressive, working at Stade Francais, Montpellier, and the Waratahs before becoming forwards coach of Australia under mentor Michael Cheika. He was coaching Argentina-based Super Rugby team the Jaguares before accepting the national job.

The challenge for Ledesma to build a squad to be reckoned with in Japan has been made easier by the decision of the Argentine

Rugby Union allowing overseas-based players to be selected in extreme circumstances, which basically means in a World Cup year. So now Ledesma could select Juan Imhoff at Racing 92, Santiago Cordero at Exeter and Toulon's Facundo Isa among others.

Ledesma is a confident coach, who is not shy in front of a microphone or television camera. Expect him to motivate his team, particularly the scrummaging unit, while enjoying the pre-match banter with opposition coaches.

PLAYERS TO WATCH

Pablo Matera is the Pumas' captain and a flanker of the modern era. He is content with using his pace and power to drive his team over the advantage line, but equally adept with a show-and-go or a perfectly weighted offload. The 26-year-old, who plays his club rugby for the Jaguares in Super Rugby and was at Leicester Tigers, has almost 60 international caps since debuting in 2013.

Matera was made captain by Ledesma in November 2018. "Pablo is a new voice and the best leader to take us where we want to go. He transmits his energy and intensity very well to the rest of the team," he said. "He reminds me of several captains that I knew, including Michael Hooper of Australia, in the way he has grown as a player."

Nicolas Sanchez is his country's highest points scorer and has made close to 80 appearances in nine years, he is truly one of the stars of the Argentinian game. He is their play-maker and ring master, and his elusive running and link-up play make him a threat to any defence in the world.

The 30-year-old fly-half plays for Stade Francais in the French Top 14 league, having previously turned out for Bordeaux and Toulon. He was also part of the Jaguares Super Rugby set-up.

After overcoming a knee injury which almost ended his rugby playing career before he was 21 years old, **Emiliano Boffelli** has gone on to be a consistent performer for Argentina since making his debut in 2017. He has impressed for the Jaguares in Super Rugby, and for the Pumas in the 2018 Rugby Championship and now has more than 20 caps.

The 24-year-old, who has played all his club rugby in Argentina, can play at fullback or wing, is solid in defence, unfazed under the high ball and known for his accuracy with long place kicks. He has proven to be a worthy replacement for Santiago Cordero who made himself unavailable for his country by choosing to play for Exeter Chiefs in the English Premiership.

Tomas Lavanini has been part of the bedrock of the Argentina squad since his selection in 2013, at the age of 20. A world class second row, Lavanini has impressed both in Super Rugby for the Jaguares and for Racing 92 in the French Top 14 league. Having recently earned his 50th international cap, it is not unrealistic for him to become the first Argentine player to make 100 appearances. His partnership with fellow lock **Guido Petti** has been a long and fruitful one for the Pumas.

Don't overlook: **Agustin Creevy**, an experienced and mobile hooker with more than 80 caps, and winger/fullback **Ramiro Moyano**, who has also represented his country at sevens.

TEAM STYLE

What style the Pumas will play in Japan will be influenced by who they are facing, but they have the capability to mix things up. Traditionally, they were a forwards-dominated team with their powerful driving pack laying the groundwork for what was to come, a typically South American trait. They relied on field position and expert kickers like Nicolas Sanchez, Hugo Porta and Gonzalo Quesada.

Now they are more comfortable with ball in hand, and allowing their backline to flourish, something which can be seen with the Jaguares in Super Rugby whose players form most of the national team. They showcased this tactical switch at the 2015 Rugby World Cup, and it was thrilling at times, but also unnecessarily reckless, failing to bring them the rewards they craved.

So, with head coach Ledesma having been one of the world's greatest hookers, don't be surprised if Argentina's scrummaging finds some new teeth and there is a return to a more cautious approach. It may not be so attractive to watch but is something with which the players are naturally comfortable.

EXPECTATIONS

Ledesma has bolstered the spirit and fortunes of the Pumas, and they seem focused on turning increasingly strong performances into test match victories. The squad should also benefit from the selection of overseas-based players and the strength and consistency in the Jaguares squad, which is the basis of the national team. Ledesma's task will be to gel these experienced players with Argentine-based ones, who play their club rugby at a lower level.

In an interview with Wales Online in May 2018, former England player and Argentina high performance manager Les Cusworth had huge expectations of the Pumas.

"Argentines are built for rugby, they have every type of athlete within their borders, they have that competitive Latin culture and are very sports savvy," he said. "Give them a level playing field in terms of opportunity and facilities and it will be a case of when, not if, they eventually win the World Cup." It would be the biggest surprise in World Cup history if they lifted the Webb Ellis Cup in Japan, but they could be the king-makers in a difficult Pool C.

Overcoming England would be a shock, but they should get the better of Tonga and the USA and will be keen to pick up crucial bonus points against these two Tier 2 nations. The contest with France, in what could be a nervous opening match, will set the tone for the pool and a positive result for the Pumas is plausible.

PREDICTION
The Pumas are likely to narrowly miss out on a quarter-final place, but it could be tantalisingly close between them and France as to who will take the Pool C runners-up spot.

ARGENTINA'S POOL C FIXTURES
France: Saturday, September 21 at Tokyo Stadium, ko 4.15pm
(GMT 7.15am)

Tonga: Saturday, September 28 at Hanazono Stadium, ko 1.45pm
(GMT 4.45am)

England: Saturday, October 5 at Tokyo Stadium, ko 5pm (GMT 8.00am)

USA: Wednesday, October 9 at Kumagaya Stadium, ko 1.45pm (GMT 4.45am)

UNITED STATES OF AMERICA

FACTS
Nickname: Eagles
World ranking: 15
Qualification: Americas 1 region champions
World Cup record: P 25, W 3, D 0, L 22
Biggest World Cup win: 39-26 against Japan (2003)
Biggest World Cup defeat: 64-0 by South Africa (2015)
World Cups – 7
Performances: Pool stage – 7

RUGBY WORLD CUP HISTORY
The USA have competed in seven of the eight World Cup tournaments. However, unlike their neighbours and rivals Canada, they have performed poorly, winning just three of their 25 matches and failing to reach the knockout stage.

For a Tier 2 nation to reach seven World Cups is an impressive feat. The only tournament the USA failed to attend was South Africa 1995, but that was understandable as it was difficult to quality for that specific competition. Canada had qualified automatically, having reached the quarter-finals in 1991, leaving Argentina, then a Tier 2 nation, and the USA to fight over the one remaining slot. The USA lost 44-33 on aggregate in the shoot-out.

The Eagles' successes have been rare but sweet, none more so than the very first one in their very first match in the very first World Cup in 1987. Tries from Purcell, Lambert and Nelson – the latter also kicking three conversions and a penalty – set up the USA for a 21-18 victory. It's been tough going since that match on May 24, 1987 with their only other wins coming in 2003 against Japan 39-26, and in 2011 against Russia 13-6. The USA often have great power in their game and have run several teams close.

In 1999, they narrowly lost 27-25 to Romania after Kurt Shuman scored a 78th minute unconverted try, and in 2003 they went down to an agonising 19-18 defeat at the hands of Fiji, despite scoring two tries to the Pacific Islanders' one. They also pushed Samoa close in 2007 before losing 26-21 – a feat they repeated in 2015 when losing 25-16, and earning praise for losing 22-10 to Ireland and 27-10 to Italy both in 2011.

History suggests that a fourth victory in a World Cup tournament is on the horizon.

BUILD-UP TO THE 2019 RUGBY WORLD CUP

In 2018, the USA won the Americas Rugby Championship for the second successive year and with it a place at Japan 2019. Gary Gold's team forced rivals Canada into the play-offs – beating them 29-10 in their Championship head-to-head en route to winning all five of their matches. The remainder of the year was promising for the Eagles who have become a honed, confident squad assisted by Major League Rugby beginning in the US which gives home-grown players access to professional rugby.

In 2018, they played seven other test matches only losing to Ireland and the Maori All Blacks. They beat Russia 62-13, Canada 42-17, Samoa 30-29, Romania 31-5 and, most memorably, Scotland 30-29 in front of 11,300 at Compass Stadium, Houston. It was the first time that the Eagles had beaten a Tier 1 nation, coming from 21-6 behind and then winning with a Hanco Germishuys try.

It capped off a memorable 2018 for the USA, however 2019 has been less impressive. Coming into the Americas Rugby Championship at the start of 2019, the Eagles were in good nick but came unstuck with lacklustre performances against an Argentina XV (45-14), who eventually claimed the title, and Uruguay (32-25) who came second. The high points were the 71-8 victory over Chile, 33-28 success over Brazil and the 30-25 win over rivals Canada. These last two only came thanks to late scores.

The USA are scheduled to compete in the 2019 World Rugby Pacific Nations Cup in July and August alongside Fiji, Tonga, Samoa, Japan and Canada as part of their final preparations for the World Cup.

HEAD COACH

Up until the start of 2019, Gary Gold appeared to have the Midas touch when it came to the USA. Gold became head coach on January 1, 2018 and from that point until the end of the Americas Rugby Championship in March 2019, the 52-year-old South African steered the Eagles to 13 victories in 17 matches. In that time, the USA qualified for the World Cup and won the 2018 Americas Rugby Championship.

Gold joined the Eagles from Worcester Warriors, in the English Premiership, taking over the job from Dave Hewlett who was a temporary replacement for fellow New Zealander John Mitchell who now works with England.

Gold's coaching career has included spells with seven clubs around the world including Western Province and Sharks in South Africa, London Irish, Warriors and Bath in England, and Kobelco Steelers in Japan. He was assistant to South Africa head coach Peter de Villiers from 2008-2011, including during the World Cup in New Zealand where the Springboks lost 11-9 to Australia in the quarter-finals.

Gold has, so far, proven to be a positive influence on the Eagles, boosting confidence levels. After his side famously beat Scotland in June 2018, the Eagles head coach told the media: "The character that was shown by this group of players was immense." He added: "I know you won't believe this is the truth, but winning or losing was not our priority, but I wanted to see how far we could progress when we played against world-class opposition."

The USA under-performed at the 2019 America Rugby Championship which may affect the squad that Gold is putting together for the World Cup.

PLAYERS TO WATCH

Blaine Scully is both a team player and leader, leaving a positive impression wherever he plays. The 31-year-old winger/fullback is close to earning 50 international caps, has enjoyed English Premiership experience with Leicester Tigers for two years and has been with Cardiff Blues since 2015.

Scully's attributes were summed up by Billy Millard, head of elite performance at Cardiff Blues, when he signed for the Welsh club. "Blaine is a determined, courageous and talented player who will add real attacking options to our back line. He is a powerful runner with a strong skill-set in the air, is strong defensively and knows how to score tries," he said.

"I was lucky to work with Blaine during my time with USA Rugby and so know the tremendous attitude, enthusiasm and professionalism he will bring with him to Cardiff Blues. He is a class act on and off the field." Just the sort of player you want as captain.

Paul Lasike is a big man with an important role to play for the Eagles at the World Cup, and he has an engaging backstory. The 29-year-old was born in Auckland but was brought up in the USA as one of 10 children born into a Tongan family of Mormon faith.

After working for a mission in Alabama, Lasike began his sporting career in the NFL, playing American football for the Arizona Cardinals and then the Chicago Bears, before switching to his first love, rugby. The 1.80m (5ft 11in) 110kg (250lb) centre was part of the Utah Warriors squad in Major League Rugby, before being signed by English Premiership side Harlequins in 2018 after an eye-catching performance in the USA's 30-29 win over Scotland.

Lasike has the potential to be a game-changer at centre for the Eagles, whether from a starting position or off the bench.

Fly-half **Alan 'AJ' MacGinty** is an influential player for the Eagles and Sale Sharks in the English Premiership but has suffered several injuries in the last 18 months. The Irish-born 29-year-old has been a part of the USA team since 2015 and has made more than 20 appearances, scoring almost 250 points.

His kicking and defensive skills are key for the Eagles. However, he followed a knee injury at the start of 2018 with a shoulder problem at the end of the year, which required surgery and a 12-week lay-off. The USA will be keen for him to be a part of their World Cup squad as he is one of the first names on the team sheet.

Prop **Titi Lamositele** has often been labelled as quiet and unassuming, but he is just content and wants his rugby do the talking. As a youth, he excelled at many sports including track and field, wrestling and American football. Despite being from a Samoan family living in Washington State, he was only introduced to rugby by chance when going to watch a friend play at school.

The 24-year-old was first selected for his country in 2013 as a teenager (becoming the youngest player at 18 to play for the Eagles) and two years later was snapped up by English Premiership side Saracens for whom he has now played more than 60 times. Lamositele was the cornerstone of the Eagles' pack at the 2015 World Cup, with both player and team benefiting from his time in elite club rugby. With youth on his side, and a growing reputation in top flight club rugby, Lamositele could again be crucial to the USA in Japan and World Cups to come.

Don't overlook: In-form flanker **Hanco Germishuys**, who has muscled **Tony Lamborn** out of the No.7 jersey, and improving hooker **Joe Taufete'e** who plays for Worcester Warriors in the English Premiership.

TEAM STYLE

The USA have power and strength throughout their squad, something which proved unstoppable in earning them the Americas Rugby Championship in 2018 and a place in Japan 2019.

After beating Canada last year, the Canucks head coach Mark Anscombe said of the USA: "They released some big guys off the bench, and we couldn't contain them. They were too big, too strong and too powerful, and in the last 20 minutes they just ran all over us."

This power game ensures that they are rarely overwhelmed, even by the most senior of Tier 1 teams, and with a good kicking game and input from their European-based stars, the Eagles can be functional or exciting as the need dictates.

The Eagles do not usually throw the ball around, as a lack of pace in the back three does not help their cause.

EXPECTATIONS

Having enjoyed unprecedented success for a majority of the last 18 months, the USA will be confident to show the world what they can do. Any victories over their pool rivals will bolster the image of the sport back in the USA, which is crucial to it expanding in this huge market. The Olympic success of the USA sevens team, and the spike in popularity for that code, has shown the potential rewards which can come from a successful World Cup tournament.

World Rugby would also be delighted to see the Eagles perform well as it looks to globally grow the game, and potentially have the USA soon host a World Cup tournament. The main negative for the Eagles in Japan is that they have been drawn in such a tough group with three Tier 1 teams and a decent Tonga side.

The USA's pool of players is growing all the time, and many perform at the highest standard overseas, so they will be competitive. Winning a single match will be a challenge but, if they do, it is likely to come against Tonga in the final pool game which could be a no-holds barred clash worth savouring.

PREDICTION

The USA may have peaked too soon and will probably finish last in Pool C, although you should expect them to leave their mark in every match that they play.

USA'S POOL C FIXTURES

England: Thursday, September 26 at Kobe Misaki Stadium, ko 7.45pm (GMT 10.45am)

France: Wednesday, October 2 at Fukuoka Hakatanomori Stadium, ko 4.45pm (GMT 7.45am)

Argentina: Wednesday, October 9 at Kumagaya Stadium, ko 1.45pm (GMT 4.45am)

Tonga: Sunday, October 13 at Hanazono Stadium, ko 2.45pm (GMT 5.45am)

TONGA

FACTS

Nickname: Ikale Tahi
World ranking: 13
Qualification: Pacific Nations Cup runners-up
World Cup record: P 25, W 7, D 0, L 18
Biggest World Cup win: 29-11 against Ivory Coast (1995)
Biggest World Cup defeat: 101-10 by England (1999)
World Cups – 7
Performances: Pool stage – 7

RUGBY WORLD CUP HISTORY

Tonga punch above their weight for an island nation with a population of approximately 110,000, of which little more than 3,000 are registered adult players. The country has produced many stars of the game, some who remain as Tongan nationals and play for the Ikale Tahi (Sea Eagles), while a growing band have qualified for New Zealand, Australia, England and other countries where the opportunities are far greater.

Despite these restrictions, Tonga have qualified for seven of the eight World Cup tournaments, only missing out on the 1991 competition, and have won 7 of their 25 matches. They are yet to advance beyond the pool stage but did come close in New Zealand in 2011, which was their most successful tournament, and included their most famous victory.

The team, coached by Isitolo Maka, lost their first Pool A match to New Zealand 41-10, before a disappointing 25-20 loss to Canada – a result which ultimately cost them the chance to appear in the knockout stage. A 31-18 victory over Japan was then followed by the upset of the tournament when they memorably triumphed over eventual champions France 19-14, fly-half Kurth Morath slotting four penalties and converting Sukanaivalu Hufanga's try to deliver victory.

Despite this, Tonga finished third in the group, two points behind France, and were eliminated. Beating France eclipsed their previous best victory which had been 28-25 over Italy in 1999.

Like 2011, the Ikale Tahi also won two matches in the 2007 tournament, finishing third in Pool A after beating rivals Samoa 19-15 and the USA 25-15. Their most recent showing at a World Cup in England 2015 produced a solitary 35-21 success over Namibia, although they pushed Georgia close before losing 17-10.

BUILD-UP TO THE 2019 RUGBY WORLD CUP

Tonga qualified for the 2019 Rugby World Cup by finishing as runners-up to Fiji in the Pacific Nations Cup in 2017, their tight 30-26 win over Samoa proving to be crucial. Since then Toutai Kefu's team have had mixed results but enjoyed a decent 25-20 win away to Romania at the end of that year and then in 2018 had the fillip of beating rivals Fiji 27-19.

However, a 74-24 setback to Wales at the Principality Stadium in the Autumn internationals underscores how difficult it always is for Tonga to overcome Tier 1 nations, something they have only achieved six times since 1973. Their players may not get together as often as other nations or have the international matches as a unit a coach may desire, but the current squad play at the highest club levels all around the world and don't lack for quality rugby.

Tonga are scheduled to compete in the 2019 World Rugby Pacific Nations Cup in July and August alongside Fiji, Samoa, Canada, Japan, and the USA. They also play New Zealand in a friendly as part of their final preparations for the World Cup.

HEAD COACH

Toutai Kefu was born in Tonga but played No.8 for Australia 60 times and was part of the 1999 World Cup-winning team. He has coached Sunshine Coast Stingrays in Australia, Kubota Spears in Japan and was Tonga's assistant coach in 2016. He combines his role as Tonga's head coach with coaching NRC team Queensland Country in Australia. With his playing and coaching experience, Kefu understands the limitations he faces with the national squad, which is adversely affected by players not available.

Some players have been adopted by other countries, capped by Tier 1 nations or made themselves unavailable in the hope of being selected by a senior nation. Kefu had hoped to strengthen his World Cup squad by selecting some former All Blacks players of Tongan descent who were scheduled to play in an Olympics Sevens tournament. However, World Rugby has now said those players – like Vaea Fifita, Charles Pitutau and Shannon Frizell – would not be qualified for Tonga.

At the end of 2018, Kefu told Stuff.co.nz of his disappointment at those who run the game globally. "I had a list of about 10-12 players who were ready to come and play for us," he said. "That gives us a good chance of making the quarter-finals in the World Cup next year. If we make the quarter-finals, that's obviously taking someone's spot. I think they are just worried about that scenario and the powerbrokers that run the game, they are represented by the Home Unions. They see us as a threat, and maybe they just don't want that competitiveness in the World Cup, which I think is very wrong."

Kefu has, though, promised that Tonga will still be 'super competitive' in Japan.

PLAYERS TO WATCH

Siale Piuatu is an experienced centre with an abrasive style, and captain of Tonga with close to 40 appearances for his country. He has played Top League in Japan with Yamaha Jubilo, and Super Rugby with New Zealand teams Chiefs and Highlanders.

After a spell with Wasps in 2016, Piuata signed for Premiership rivals Bristol Bears in 2017 where he has played more than 30 matches. Bears head coach Pat Lam has described 33-year-old Piuata in glowing terms. After his contract was extended at the end of 2018, Lam said of Piuata: "He brings nous and physicality to our game and is one of our leaders, on and off the field."

His younger brother Charles, who has played for the All Blacks, is also a Bristol Bears player but can't play for Tonga yet because three years has not elapsed since his last New Zealand match.

Sonatane Takulua, who has also worn the captain's armband, is 28 years old and a pivotal player for Tonga and his club Newcastle Falcons at scrum-half. Falcons director of rugby Dean Richards said Takulua plays 'with a smile on his face' and is at the 'peak of his powers,' adding: "He is a top international-quality scrum-half who has shown he is capable of a consistently high level of performance."

Valentino Mapalangi is a versatile player who performs in the back row for Tonga and Leicester Tigers, but can fill in at second row. The 26-year-old has impressed at Leicester in the English Premiership although 2018 saw his game time restricted by numerous injuries. He has played for Tonga since 2015 and could be a star in the making if he remains injury-free.

"Representing Tonga means everything to me, because you're representing your family and all those people back home," he said at the end of 2018. Mapalangi still has plenty to prove to secure a starting position with Tonga but, given the chance, Japan 2019 could be his time to shine.

Paul Ngauamo is a consistent performer for Tonga as hooker since debuting in 2014, with his strength and technical ability being strong assets. Born in New Zealand to Tongan parents, he hit the headlines for all the wrong reasons in the 2015 World Cup. After a dangerous tackle in the pool match against the All Blacks, he received a three-week suspension.

Ngauamo, 29, has played for Agen in the French Top 14 league since 2017 and is a popular member of the squad, known for his one-liners and quick wit. In an interview with Rugby World, when asked about the silliest thing he'd ever bought, Ngauamo replied: "A salad."

Don't overlook: Consistent fly-half **Latiume Fosita**, and experienced winger **Alaska Taufa**.

TEAM STYLE

Similar to Samoa, Tonga's approach to most games will be built around the power of their players, regardless of the position they play. They revel in the contact side of the game, seeking it out where possible, and looking to wear down their opponents.

They have skill and energy, but often revert to type, crashing into defences at pace to create weaknesses which can be exploited. This can be an effective weapon against some junior nations, but is difficult to maintain against Tier 1 teams, many whom have Pacific Islanders playing for them, and are used to the physicality of the modern game. But this won't stop Tonga from trying and, for fans of big one-up hits and monster tackling, Tonga are always a must-watch.

EXPECTATIONS

Tonga will expect to win at least one match in Pool C, most likely against a USA team which will also view this contest as winnable. England, France and Argentina will be difficult opponents, as are all Tier 1 nations for Tonga.

They beat Fiji for the first time in seven years mid-way through 2018 but ended the campaign with a 74-24 thrashing at the hands of Wales, highlighting the Tongans' issues against senior teams. It would be a major surprise if this form changed at the World Cup.

Tonga have the players to be a global force, but the finances of the game mean that most elect to play for New Zealand or elsewhere. There will be plenty of players at the World Cup who are Tongan-born or of Tongan descent, but not all will be playing for the Ikale Tahi.

Coach Toutai Kefu has been trying to tempt some back into the Tongan fold, but this will not bolster the squad in time for the World Cup. Tonga will be competitive and could leave a mental and physical mark on some players in the Tier 1 teams.

But don't expect them to cause an upset, and instead just revel in watching a small island nation summon up the warrior spirit to go toe-to-toe with anyone who stands in their way and enjoy doing it.

PREDICTION
A victory over the USA will see them finish fourth in Pool C, something they are more than capable of achieving. Anything more will be a surprise.

TONGA'S POOL C FIXTURES
England: Sunday, September 22 at Sapporo Dome, ko 7.15pm (GMT 10.15am)

Argentina: Saturday, September 28 at Hanazono Stadium, ko 1.45pm (GMT 4.45am)

France: Sunday, October 6 at Kumamoto Stadium, ko 4.45pm (GMT 7.45am)

USA: Sunday, October 13 at Hanazono Stadium, ko 2.45pm (GMT 5.45am)

POOL D

AUSTRALIA

FACTS
Nickname: Wallabies
World ranking: 6
Qualification: Automatic (winners of Pool A in RWC 2015)
World Cup record: P 48, W 39, D 0, L 9
Biggest World Cup win: 142-0 against Namibia (2003)
Biggest World Cup defeat: 34-17 by New Zealand (2015)
World Cups – 8
Performances: Champions – 2; runners-up – 2; third place – 1; fourth place – 1; quarter-finals – 2

RUGBY WORLD CUP HISTORY
In the eight Rugby World Cups to date, the Wallabies have been crowned champions twice, reached four finals in total and made the semi-finals six times making them, by any measure, one of the game's big-hitters and a side who will raise their game come competition time.

They rarely underperform in the tournament. Yet their two triumphs came in the 1990s, with both being in the Northern Hemisphere.

Their 1991 success was perhaps their most memorable if only for the number of close matches Australia edged, despite having world class players like John Eales, Michael Lynagh, Tim Horan and David Campese.

Having won their pool, although they almost came unstuck against Western Samoa who they narrowly beat 9-3, Australia played an attractive form of the game to beat Ireland 19-18 in a dramatic quarter-final, and New Zealand 16-6 in the semi-finals. Tony Daly scored the only try in the final against England at Twickenham, which Australia won 12-6.

They lifted the Webb Ellis Cup for a second time in 1999 and this time were rarely tested. Having romped past Romania, Ireland and the USA in the pool stage, Australia beat hosts Wales 24-9 in the quarter-final before a classic semi-final against South Africa. Australia won 27-21 after extra-time in a match which featured 14 penalties and 2 drop goals. They eased past France 35-12 in the final with Ben Tune and Owen Finegan scoring tries, and Mathew Burke slotting seven penalties.

The Wallabies were beaten finalists in 2003 on home soil, losing 20-17 in the final to England after Jonny Wilkinson clipped over a late drop goal, and in 2015, when they lost to a formidable All Blacks team in the final. The 34-17 defeat is the heaviest loss the Wallabies have suffered in their World Cup history.

Even though rugby union competes against other sports in their own country with higher profiles, such as Australian rules football and rugby league, the Wallabies continue to produce some of the best players in the world who peak for the World Cup every four years.

BUILD-UP TO THE 2019 RUGBY CUP

The Rugby Championship, which takes place in the middle of the calendar year between Australia, New Zealand, Argentina and

South Africa, has taken on a familiar pattern with the Wallabies underperforming while the All Blacks take the title. This has been the case for the past four years, and in 2018 this form continued as Australia finished third with two wins and four losses, one of those setbacks being 23-19 to Argentina on the Gold Coast.

The remainder of the calendar year witnessed the Wallabies lose 2-1 in a three-test match series at home to Ireland and then go down 37-20 in the final Bledisoe Cup match against New Zealand, a contest played in Japan at the Rugby World Cup final venue.

The Northern Hemisphere tour at the end of the year was equally as unpromising with a 26-7 victory over Italy, sandwiched between a 9-6 defeat to Wales and a 37-18 loss to England. That last defeat at Twickenham was the sixth consecutive they have suffered at the hands of their old adversaries. Australia lost 11 of their 15 test matches in 2018 and are out of sorts in the build-up to the World Cup, but head coach Michael Cheika tried to put this year into context.

He said: "I love footie and you can't just have the good bits. We've felt sad often and we've felt pain often, but we will use that when we come back. There are a lot of great people in our team and a lot of great things happening behind the scenes that right now aren't turning themselves into wins, but we will turn them into wins next year (2019)."

In July and August this year, Australia are scheduled to play three matches in the shortened Rugby Championship against South Africa, Argentina and New Zealand. The Wallabies then meet the All Blacks again in the Bledisoe Cup, and Samoa in their final World Cup warm-up match.

HEAD COACH

Michael Cheika, 52, is head coach of Australia and has been since 2014, making him one of the longest serving coaches in the international game. He was seen as the ideal man to take over from Ewen MacKenzie, who unexpectedly resigned, and is the only man to have ever won the elite club competition in each hemisphere, taking the Heineken Cup with Leinster in 2009 and the Super Rugby title with Waratahs in 2014.

In 2015, he led the Wallabies to the Rugby Championship and the final of the World Cup, ending the year being named World Rugby Coach of the Year. Since then Cheika, the son of Lebanese migrants to Australia, has struggled to maintain the team's form and his success rate with the Wallabies is currently just under 50 percent.

The defeat to Argentina in 2018 led many ex-players to call for him to be sacked, and he is sometimes seen as a distant figure by the public. But after a review, he kept a hold of his job and now reports to Scott Johnson, who was brought into the new role of director of rugby.

He is not one to veer away from sharing his opinion in public, particularly when it comes to contentious decisions by referees, and his fiery nature has often led to run-ins with authority. In an interview with the Sydney Morning Herald in March this year, Cheika played the underdog card as he looked ahead to the World Cup.

"We've got ourselves a good plan for building momentum this year, I think that's really important for us," he said. "There are some things we might add into our game, on both sides of the ball, and start building ourselves some momentum and try to catch teams underestimating us a little bit. We will be going into all the tournaments this year – the Rugby Championship and World Cup – as underdogs and we've got to take advantage of that."

PLAYERS TO WATCH

Michael Hooper is a tough, dynamic flanker and captain of an Australian team which desperately needs the leadership he provides. Despite being in a struggling pack which can be out-muscled and not being the physically biggest of back row players, Cooper often shines with his all-action approach.

The 28-year-old from Sydney, whose father is English, played in Super Rugby for the Brumbies before moving to the Waratahs in 2013, and has been a Wallabies player since making his debut in 2012. He has earned an excess of 90 international caps and been recognised for his leadership skills by twice being named Wallaby of the Year by the Aussie fans. His presence on and off the pitch will be important if Australia are to overcome recent poor form and the challenge for a third Webb Ellis Cup.

Will Genia has been one of the most high-profile scrum-halves in the world since he debuted for the Wallabies in 2009. The diminutive No.9, who was born in Papua New Guinea, has played more than 100 times for his country and is known for his strength. During team bench press testing in 2011, Genia recorded two repetitions of 180kg – more than twice his body weight. Explosive power and a low centre of gravity are key to his impressive defensive capabilities and line-breaking pace.

The popular Genia played 114 times for Queensland Reds in the Super Rugby championship where he struck up a productive partnership with fly-half **Quade Cooper**, which carried on through to the international arena. Their careers took separate paths for a few years; however, the two friends are now back playing side by side for Super Rugby franchise Melbourne Rebels, prompting calls for this half-back partnership to again represent their country together.

Former Wallabies captain **David Pocock** is a man known for his integrity and commitment. The 31-year-old flanker or No.8 was born in Zimbabwe, but the family moved to Australia in 2002 because of civil unrest in his homeland. He joined Perth-based Western Force in the Super Rugby league in 2006, earning the first of his almost 80 international caps that year. He joined the Brumbies in 2013 and has excelled for them but has also been set back on many occasions by injuries, leading to him having to shift his position for the Wallabies, as Michael Hooper came through the ranks.

He shines in the contact area, winning penalties and turnovers, and is tough to move when he gets over the ball because of his strength. Pocock's reputation rose higher after tending to an injured opponent while the match continued, and for delaying marriage to his fiancé for eight years until same-sex marriage was legalised in Australia.

Pocock and Hooper, known collectively in Australia as 'Pooper', are the mainstay of the back row, but this experienced pairing could be challenged by **Isi Naisarani**, a 24-year-old Fijian who has just been given Australian citizenship.

Known as 'the Iceman,' **Bernard Foley** can cover both fullback and fly-half and is known for his place kicking under pressure. His impressive international record of more than 600 points in around 70 matches, and experience of playing Super Rugby for the Waratahs and time spent in Japan with the Ricoh Black Rams, makes him a vital cog in the Wallabies' machine.

He has cemented the No.10 playmaker position for himself ahead of the World Cup, and recently suggested that members of the Wallabies squad should be rested for some Super Rugby matches – in line with New Zealand's approach – to keep the players fresh for the World Cup.

Don't overlook: **Rob Simmons**, the hard-working lock with more than 90 caps, and experienced centre **Kurtley Beale,** who is an important part of Australia's midfield.

TEAM STYLE

Australia play to their strength which has always been, and remains, a creative, entertaining backline which can slice through defences at a pace that is just hard to match. Strike runners and inventive play-makers have been at the heart of Australian rugby, and its players, such as Bernard Foley and Adam Ashley-Cooper, on whom the Wallabies will be pinning much of their hopes.

However, confidence plays a large part in being able to make this style of rugby successful, and Australia are currently still a work in progress when it comes to this aspect of their game. Building confidence takes time, but this is something which is running out for the Wallabies.

Although head coach Cheika is known for favouring a strong pack from which to build a platform, this area remains the team's Achilles' heel, and where they suffer in comparison to many of their rivals.

EXPECTATIONS

Unless the Wallabies come into the tournament off the back of some encouraging victories in the Rugby Championship in July and August, or at least some success for their Super Rugby club teams – which feature their international players – the chances of them adding to their haul of World Cup triumphs seem remote.

The coach, players and Australian media are already positioning themselves as plucky underdogs which tells you all you need to know about the low expectations surrounding the squad.

The Wallabies' hopes were further dented in April when the country's governing body, Rugby Australia, sacked star player Israel Folau after he posted homophobic messages on social media. However, Australia retain world class match-winners and are in a pool from which they would normally expect to progress.

Reaching the semi-finals would be a major surprise for a team with little form over the past two years but would confirm that the Wallabies still have the game to win one-off matches as they have done in past tournaments.

PREDICTION

The Wallabies will have to shift up a gear just to find the form they require to safely progress out of the pool, while getting past the quarter-finals will be a major achievement for the self-styled underdogs.

AUSTRALIA'S POOL D FIXTURES

Fiji: Saturday, September 21 at Sapporo Dome, ko 1.45pm (GMT 4.45am)

Wales: Sunday, September 29 at Tokyo Stadium, ko 4.45pm (GMT 7.45am)

Uruguay: Saturday, October 5 at Oita Stadium, ko 2.15pm (GMT 5.15am)

Georgia: Friday, October 11 at Shizuoka Stadium, ko 7.15pm (GMT 10.15am)

WALES

FACTS

Nickname: None
World ranking: 2
Qualification: Automatic (Runners-ups in Pool A in RWC 2015)
World Cup record: P 37, W 21, D 0, L 16
Biggest World Cup win: 81-7 against Namibia (2007)
Biggest World Cup defeat: 49-6 by New Zealand (1987)
World Cups – 8
Performances: Third place – 1; fourth place – 1; quarter-finals – 3; pool stage – 3

RUGBY WORLD CUP HISTORY

For a Tier 1 nation which lives and breathes rugby, and which has produced some of the finest players ever to grace the game, Wales are perennial World Cup under-performers. They have played in all eight tournaments, but only twice reached the semi-finals. They have failed to progress out of the pool stage three times.

The first World Cup in 1987 proved to be their most successful even though they came into it in poor form. Head coach Tony Gray steered his side to a third-place finish after beating Australia 22-21 in the bronze medal match with Gareth Roberts, William Moriarty, and Adrian Hadley scoring tries in addition to the points kicked by Paul Thorburn. It was to be another 24 years before Wales would reach the semi-finals again, this time under head coach Warren Gatland.

The 2011 tournament saw them lose narrowly 17-16 to South Africa in Pool A before beating Samoa 17-10, Namibia 81-7 and Fiji 66-0. They overcame Ireland 22-10 in the quarters before losing 9-8 in a classic semi to France, despite Mike Phillips scoring the only try of the match, and 21-18 to the Wallabies in the bronze medal match.

In the years in between the two semi-final appearances, Wales played their part in some historic matches but, highlighting their image as the nearly-men of World Cup tournaments, the results went against them.

They lost 16-13 to Western Samoa in 1991 in a dramatic match that decided which team would progress from the pool behind Australia. They went down 24-23 to Ireland in 1995, suffered again at the hands of Samoa in 1999, but still progressed despite the 38-31 setback, and again missed out on a quarter-final spot after a 38-34 defeat by Fiji. In 2015, they lost 23-19 to South Africa in the quarters, but before that enjoyed the immense satisfaction of knocking out hosts England in the pool stage after a famous 28-25 victory at Twickenham.

BUILD-UP TO THE 2019 RUGBY CUP

Wales certainly finished 2018 on the front foot with seven consecutive victories, after finishing second in the Six Nations following defeats to England and Ireland. Warren Gatland's squad won all three test matches on their tour of Argentina during the summer and then overcame Scotland 21-10, Australia 9-6, Tonga 74-24 and South Africa 20-11 in the autumn internationals.

An impressive set of results set them up for a successful tilt at the 2019 Six Nations, which they won with a Grand Slam performance. By the end of the tournament, in which they were not always at their best but found a way to win, they had overcome France 24-19, Italy 26-15, England 21-13, Scotland 18-11 and Ireland 25-7, extending their winning run to a mighty 14 matches.

Wales are scheduled to have home and away clashes with both England and Ireland in August and early September as warm-up games for the World Cup.

HEAD COACH

New Zealander Warren Gatland became head coach of Wales in 2007 after the sacking of Gareth Jenkins whose side failed to perform at that year's World Cup.

Gatland, who has led Wales in more than 100 test matches, announced that he will leave his post at the end of Japan 2019 after 12 years in charge. The 56-year-old has said he plans to return to his native New Zealand, although he will not be short of job offers from nations and clubs around the world.

Gatland is an experienced coach whose clubs have included Connaught in Ireland, Wasps in England and Waikato in New Zealand. He coached the British and Irish Lions on tours to Australia in 2013 and New Zealand in 2017, and was head coach of Ireland from 1998-2001, all with varying degrees of success. He has said his style is to empower players, to build trust and loyalty and not dominate as head coach.

While it's the coach's job to develop the structure, he believes that senior players are the real drivers of discipline and the quality of training, and the setting of standards and goals. He has successfully overhauled Wales in the last 18 months from a team based on a more structured style of play to one which is more dynamic and open. The strength in depth of the current squad has also allowed him to make this change, something that he acknowledges.

Gatland led Wales to Six Nations success in 2019 – the third time he has achieved this feat – but will crave World Cup glory before he heads off to his next challenge.

PLAYERS TO WATCH
Alun Wyn Jones is a formidable opponent, an inspirational captain and an unofficial ambassador for all that is right with the game of rugby.

The 33-year-old second row from Swansea has played for Welsh side Ospreys since they were formed in 2005, amassing almost 250 appearances. His Wales debut came the following year and his number of international caps is in excess of 120, making him the world's most capped lock forward. He has also represented the British and Irish Lions nine times.

He is known for his tireless and intelligent approach on the pitch, but also for rousing his team-mates when the going is tough, often merely by his presence. A lot of what he adds to the Wales squad is unseen by those outside the dressing room. He was named 2019 Six Nations player of the tournament.

George North is not one to take a backward step when confronted by a challenge, and not one to rest on his laurels. North was at Scarlets in Wales for two seasons before joining English Premiership side Northampton Saints in 2013. Last year, he returned to Wales when he signed for Ospreys.

North is a Welsh speaker and proud Welshman, but was born in England, to an English father and Welsh mother, before moving to Anglesey at the age of two. At 1.94m (6ft 4in) and 109kg (169lb), this mobile Welsh mountain of a man is fearless and committed with or without the ball, although his contact-heavy style has led to issues with concussions, five in two years at one stage.

The powerful 27-year-old wing has achieved much on the rugby pitch and is en route to becoming the leading try scorer for Wales, a run which began with him scoring on his debut in 2010 at the age of 18. He has already played more than 80 times for Wales and is a key presence in the squad.

Taulope Faletau endured a frustrating and painful end to 2018 after fracturing his forearm and then suffering the same injury on his return to the game in January 2019, forcing him to miss the Six Nations. It was another cruel blow to the world class No.8 but will make him even more determined to succeed at the World Cup, assuming he can remain injury free.

The Tongan-born powerhouse, who moved to Wales with his family at the age of seven, has played more than 70 times in eight seasons for Wales, represented Newport Gwent Dragons in excess of 100 times, and has also been capped by the British and Irish Lions. Known for his mobility and laser-guided tackling, if Faletau – affectionately called Toby by those in the game – hits his straps in Japan, then Wales will be a considerable threat.

Jonathan Davies is a big-game player and one of the best midfielders in the world. Known as Foxy, the 31-year-old is one of the first names down on the Wales team sheet, as he would be for most nations. Born in England to Welsh parents, the centre has played most of his club rugby for Scarlets, although he has had two seasons at both Llanelli and Clermont Auvergne.

He has earned more than 70 caps for Wales and has represented the British and Irish Lions, being named their player of the tour of New Zealand in 2017 by his team-mates. Davies is athletic, has a wicked turn of pace to skirt around any defence, enviable handling skills and is technically correct; he's a textbook centre.

Don't overlook**: Liam Williams**, a gifted if injury prone fullback, and **Justin Tipuric**, an intelligent and dangerous open side flanker.

TEAM STYLE

Throughout the 60s, 70s and even 80s, Wales were known for their crowd-pleasing backs and ability and willingness to run the ball from anywhere on the park. It was this type of rugby which made household names of Barry John, Gareth Edwards, JPR Williams, Jonathan Davies, and Ieuan Evans. However, a dearth of quality playmakers, coupled with Warren Gatland's instincts, initially led Wales to be a more structured, forwards-dominated team with mixed results. It has been termed 'Warrenball'.

The Wales of today, as witnessed in the 2019 Six Nations, is more of a throwback to the golden era when the backs were the stars, even if they are now built like powerlifters and prefer to crash through, rather than glide around, defences. The strength in depth Wales now possess has allowed Gatland to make this switch, one which has made them an attractive team to watch and appreciate. With quality players primed and ready on the side lines, like the game-changing Dan Biggar, Wales have a true impact bench. All these ingredients make Wales a force on the world rugby stage.

EXPECTATIONS

The turbo-charged, super-confident Wales team are one of the front-runners to lift the Webb Ellis Cup. Their ruthless form to the end of the Six Nations, the star quality and depth of their squad, the experience of their coaching set-up and the attractive brand of rugby they play can only lead to that conclusion.

The coaches and players might not want to hear it, and the long-suffering fans, who have travelled the globe hoping against hope for World Cup success, may only dream it, but it's a fact. If Wales can reproduce their A-game on enough occasions, they can win Pool D and any knockout matches which come their way.

Before his team won the Six Nations, Warren Gatland said that he hoped Wales could go to Japan 'under the radar'. There is no chance of that now. Success has forced Gatland and players like Gareth Anscombe to come out and proudly admit that Wales are potential World Cup winners. For the first time in many years, Wales are right to have such high expectations.

PREDICTION
Wales have forgotten how to lose, especially in the big games, and appear to have peaked at the optimum time leaving few to question their credentials as potential World Cup winners.

WALES' FIXTURES IN POOL D
Georgia: Monday, September 23 at City of Toyota Stadium, ko 7.15pm (GMT 10.15am)

Wales: Sunday, September 29 at Tokyo Stadium, ko 4.45pm (GMT 7.45am)

Fiji: Wednesday, October 9 at Oita Stadium, ko 6.45pm (GMT 9.45am)

Uruguay: Sunday, October 13 at Kumamoto Stadium, ko 5.15pm (GMT 8.15am)

GEORGIA

FACTS
Nickname: Lelos
World ranking: 12
Qualification: Automatic (third place in Pool C in RWC 2015)
World Cup record: P 16, W 4, D 0, L 12
Biggest World Cup win: 30-0 against Namibia (2007)
Biggest World Cup defeat: 84-6 by England (2003)
World Cups – 4
Performances: Pool stage – 4

RUGBY WORLD CUP HISTORY
Georgia's history at the Rugby World Cup is short, but for a country which only played their first international match as an independent nation in 1989, it's impressive and constantly improving.

Rugby was introduced to Georgia in the late 1950s and has now grown to become one of the country's most popular sports, thanks to substantial investment from their government, billionaire and former Prime Minister Bidzine Ivanishvili, and its similarity to an old Georgian sport called lelo burti. Georgia became a member of World Rugby in 1992 and have grown to become a power in the Rugby Europe Championships.

The first World Cup for the Lelos was in 2003, which they began by losing 84-6 to eventual champions England, a result which is still Georgia's biggest defeat in the tournament. From this low point, they improved steadily although their first success did not come until 2007 when, after narrowly losing 14-10 to Ireland, they overcame Namibia 30-0 with tries from Akvsent Guiorgadze, Irakil Machkaneli, and Davit Kacharava.

New Zealand 2011 was another tournament where lessons were learned for the Lelos who beat Romania 25-9, and only lost narrowly to Scotland (15-6) and Argentina (25-7). Georgia qualified for their fourth consecutive World Cup in 2015 and, in line with their growing confidence as a rugby nation, it proved to be their most successful. They finished third in Pool C – and so for the first time automatically qualified for the next World Cup tournament in Japan.

The pool matches began with a 17-10 victory over Tonga – Mamuka Gorgodze and Giga Tkhilaishvili scoring tries – and ended with a nail-biting 17-16 success over Namibia in which Gorgodze and Lasha Malaghuradze dotted down. In between, they went down 54-9 to Argentina and 43-10 to England, but it was all another big step forward for the scrappy eastern Europeans who are eager to sit at rugby's top table.

BUILD-UP TO THE 2019 RUGBY WORLD CUP

Georgia lost 28-17 to Italy in Florence last November in the first match between the two nations for 15 years. This was followed by wins over tourists Samoa (27-19) and Tonga (20-9) in Tbilisi. This set them up for the defence of the Rugby Europe Championship at the start of 2019 as did a behind-closed-doors practice match with England, during which it was reported that two fights broke out between both sets of forwards.

All this proved fruitful for Georgia who succeeded in winning the Rugby Europe Championship for the 10th time in the last 12 years. They beat Romania 18-9, Spain 24-10, Belgium 46-6, Germany 52-3, and Russia 22-6 to maintain their dominance in the tournament also known as the Six Nations B championship.

As part of their World Cup run-in, the Lelos are scheduled to face Russia and Scotland in Tbilisi in August, before heading to Murrayfield in early September to clash with Scotland again.

HEAD COACH

Milton Haig is just the fifth head coach the Lelos have employed since 2000, and the second New Zealander after Tim Lane, although there has also been a Frenchman, a Georgian and a Scotsman. Haig, 55, has been in charge since 2011 and has overseen almost 80 matches of which two-thirds have ended in victory for Georgia.

Having enjoyed coaching experience with more than 10 teams including New Zealand Under-21s, Maori All Blacks and the Chiefs in Super Rugby, Haig took the role with Georgia and led them to seven Rugby Europe Championship titles, along with qualification for the 2015 and 2019 World Cups. He is driving Georgian rugby forward and has said on numerous occasions that he hopes to oversee the country's entry into the Six Nations. However, that still seems to be a long way off even though Georgia are ranked 12th in the world, while Six Nations strugglers Italy are ranked 14th.

Under Haig, assisted by former England forwards coach Graham Rowntree, Georgia have maintained their position as the best team in Europe outside the Six Nations teams, and are hard to beat, fiercely contesting every set piece.

PLAYERS TO WATCH

Merab Sharikadze was born in Russia, educated in England, plays club rugby in France for Aurillac, and is captain of Georgia.

The centre, known for his tackling prowess, made his debut for Georgia at the age of 18 in 2012 and has amassed more than 60 caps.

Sharikadze's star shone bright at the 2015 World Cup, especially in the narrow 17-16 victory over Namibia when he kicked flawlessly in making seven points, tackled hard and beat nine defenders with his intelligent lines of running during the match. The 25-year-old has risen to the challenge of taking over the captain's armband from Mamuka Gorgodze, a player he has called a 'great player and captain'.

Tighthead prop **Levan Chilachava** is a formidable opponent, especially in the scrum, whether it's for Georgia or for club side Montpelier who he joined in 2018 after six successful years at Top 14 side Toulon, where he was a permanent fixture in their front row.

The 28-year-old, who made his international debut in 2012 and has nearly 50 caps, will be eager to perform well in Georgia's mighty pack in Japan, after having to pull out of the previous World Cup in England with a muscle tear. This battle-scarred warrior encapsulates the power and commitment of the Georgian team.

Merab Kvirikashvili is a record-breaker for Georgia with more caps, almost 120, and more points, almost 850, than any other player. The World Cup could be his last hurrah. Although he no longer has the kicking duties for Georgia, the 35-year-old fullback is an experienced member of the Lelos squad.

His presence in and around the team, and in the dressing room, will still be important for Georgia even if the amount of game-time he is given is diminishing. Kvirikashvili played club rugby in France for 11 years and has also represented his country in rugby league and sevens.

Mikheil Nariashvili has the credentials to be considered the best loose head prop in the world, another reason for Georgia's deserved reputation as set piece masters.

It is in the scrum that he puts in his biggest shifts, but he is a fine ball carrier in the loose and has an enviable work rate for a player of his size. He has played for Georgia more than 50 times, and more than 135 times for Top 14 team Montpellier since joining them in 2010.

Don't overlook: Feisty scrum-half **Vasil Lobzhanidze**, who has more than 40 caps, and 22-year-old flanker **Giorgi Tsutskiridze**, who plays for Aurillac in France.

TEAM STYLE

England coach Eddie Jones has said that Georgia have 'the biggest, ugliest, strongest scrum pack in the world'. More than any other international team, it's the forwards who are the pin-up boys of the Georgian game, and who are the power which drives their set-piece based approach.

Georgian players relish the physical aspects of the sport and, with most playing their club rugby in France or England, get to show what they can do at the highest level. They carry the ball into contact areas with no qualms as that is where they can show off their rucking and mauling skills.

Away from the contact areas, the coaches are trying to address the team's deficiencies outside the pack. In an interview with CNN, head coach Milton Haig said: "Really our game was based around the forwards. I don't think that's going to be the same in Japan. One of the things now is we've developed a lot of young players. The team likes to play with a bit more width."

That may be the hope but, in the short term, the forwards remain the rock stars and the backs the back-up singers.

EXPECTATIONS

Forwards coach Graham Rowntree has said he wants Georgia to be 'spoken about' at the World Cup and to 'scare' teams, he has also commented about how Tier 1 teams – like Australia and Wales in Pool D – will be under pressure to beat Georgia, something his players can exploit. The closest the Lelos have come to beating a top team was in 2007 when they lost 14-10 to Ireland, and so it would be the greatest day in Georgian rugby if they were to overcome either of the big two in Pool D.

Despite their improvements in the last decade, this type of result is unlikely, but remains an aim for a focused team. More likely is that Georgia will beat Uruguay and then tussle with Fiji to see who claims the important third place which comes with automatic qualification to the 2023 World Cup.

Both teams normally hold sway on home soil, so this clash in neutral Japan between a structured Georgia and a more carefree Fiji could be the most tense but exciting contest of Pool D. Defeat in this match would be a huge disappointment for Georgia and an under-achievement at a time when they are pushing the world of rugby to admit them to the exclusive Tier 1 nations club.

PREDICTION
A fourth-place finish in Pool D for a committed Georgia team whose best is still ahead of them.

GEORGIA'S POOL D FIXTURES
Wales: Monday, September 23 at City of Tokyo Stadium, ko 7.15pm (GMT 10.15am)

Uruguay: Sunday, September 29 at Kumagaya Stadium, ko 2.15pm (GMT 5.15am)

Fiji: Thursday, October 3 at Hanazono Stadium, ko 2.15pm (GMT 5.15am)

Australia: Friday, October 11 at Shizuoka Stadium, ko 7.15pm (GMT 10.15am)

FIJI

FACTS
Nickname: Flying Fijians
World ranking: 9
Qualification: Oceania region champions
World Cup record: P 28, W 10, D 0, L 18
Biggest World Cup win: 67-18 against Namibia (1999)
Biggest World Cup defeat: 66-0 by Wales (2011)

World Cups – 7
Performances: Quarter-finals – 2; quarter-final play-offs – 1; pool stage – 4

RUGBY WORLD CUP HISTORY

For a country with a population of fewer than 1 million people, of which approximately 80,00 are registered players, Fiji have performed admirably at World Cup tournaments of which they have qualified for seven out of eight. This small Pacific island nation has won 10 of their 28 matches, and played an exciting, vibrant brand of rugby which few can match. If more of their home-grown talent made themselves available for their country, as opposed to switching allegiances to play in New Zealand or Europe, the Flying Fijians may have enjoyed more than the limited success which has come their way.

The country's sevens team are Olympic champions and perhaps the finest in the world, and the 15-a-side team attempt to play in the same joyous manner but are yet to progress beyond the World Cup quarter-finals.

Their most impressive campaign came in 2007 when they were drawn in a pool with Australia and Wales – as they have been for the 2019 tournament – as well as Japan and Canada. They beat Japan 31-35, and Canada 29-16, and then lost 55-12 to Australia, leaving their clash with Wales to decide which of the two teams would progress. In what is one of the greatest World Cup matches of all time, Fiji won a see-saw affair 38-34 to reach the quarter-finals. Although the Fijians lost 37-20 to South Africa in the knockout stage, the tournament was, and still is, their most impressive to date and is fondly remembered at home. Fiji also reached the quarter-finals in 1987 and the play-offs for the last eight in 1999. The only time they failed to qualify was in 1995.

Last time out, in 2015, Fiji could only win once, beating Uruguay, but were competitive in a tough pool where they narrowly lost to hosts England (35-11), Australia (28-13) and Wales (23-13).

BUILD-UP TO THE 2019 RUGBY WORLD CUP

Last year produced a typically mixed bag of results for Fiji as they tried to find some momentum heading into a World Cup year. They won their fourth consecutive Pacific Nations Cup in 2018, ensuring the title after coming from behind to beat Georgia 37-16, but their initial match of the competition against Samoa was a nail-biter which they finally won 24-22. This was followed up by a one-off clash with Tonga, which they lost 27-19 on home soil. This was the first time the Flying Fijians had lost to rivals Tonga in seven years – not exactly the morale boost they craved.

A 54-17 defeat to Scotland and 68-7 victory over Uruguay in England followed, before they ended the year on a memorable high with an historic 21-14 success over France in Paris. Semi Radradra and Josua Tuisvola scored tries and Ben Volavola kicked 11 points as Fiji came from 14-12 down at half-time to win, recording a rare victory over a Tier 1 team and their first ever over France. The Fijians fell to their knees in prayer at the end of the match.

Fiji are scheduled to compete in the 2019 World Rugby Pacific Nations Cup in July and August alongside Samoa, Tonga, Canada, Japan and the USA as part of their final preparations for the World Cup. They will enjoy a rare extended period together as a squad which should be a huge positive ahead of the World Cup.

HEAD COACH

New Zealander John McKee moved from being Fiji's high-performance unit manager to head coach in 2014 and in his initial match steered them to a 25-14 success over Italy – a first victory over a Tier 1 side in seven years. He capped an encouraging year with Fiji securing qualification to the 2015 Rugby World Cup by beating Cook Islands 108-6.

The former AS Montferrand, Connaught, Cornish Pirates, Central Coast Rays and Australia Under-20s coach has since guided Fiji to four Pacific Nations titles (up to and including 2018 which earned qualification for Japan 2019) and a commendable showing at the last World Cup. He has also presided over Fijian victories against Tier 1 nations Italy (22-19) and Scotland (27-22), and a narrow 23-20 defeat to Ireland, all in 2017.

As with all coaches of Pacific Island nations, McKee has the challenge of players either having switched allegiances to other countries, or who play in Europe and are not always available because of club commitments. He has said he believes the country has some of the most talented players in the world and having a Pacific Island franchise in Super Rugby would keep more players in the Fiji fold.

The country currently has a team – Fijian Drua – in the Australian National Rugby Championship which is helping younger players gain more exposure to senior rugby and enhanced coaching. Fiji are also in a slightly healthier financial position than their Pacific Island rivals, which leads McKee to be an optimist looking ahead.

In an interview with the Ireland edition of the Independent in 2017, the head coach said: "We are really working towards putting together a team and a support staff that makes sure we put ourselves in the best position to try and get out of our pool and to the play-offs.

"If we were to play the World Cup today, we couldn't achieve that because we're not there yet but the work we can do over the next two years, I believe that with the talent of players we've got, we can achieve that."

PLAYERS TO WATCH

Ben Volavola is Fiji's exciting fly-half who, at 28 years old, has a wealth of experience behind him and many years of top-flight rugby ahead. Born in Australia to an Indian father and Fijian mother, Volavola played for Australia Under-20s before being selected by Fiji for whom he has scored around 180 points in 30 appearances.

Volavola was signed by French Top 14 side Racing 92 from Bordeaux-Begles but has also played for clubs in Australia and New Zealand including Super Rugby sides Waratahs, Crusaders and Rebels. He is a pivotal player for Fiji with his athletic approach to the fly-half spot, intelligent kicking and deceptive pace.

Vereniki Goneva has made an impact wherever, and for whoever, he has played. At centre, or sometimes on the wing, he is a phenomenal sight in full flight, causing nightmares for defences around the world with his raw pace and power.

The 35-year-old has played for Fiji since 2007, breaking the 50-cap barrier and scoring more than 100 points. He has played club rugby in France, but it is England where he has enjoyed most of his success. He played 79 times for Leicester Tigers, and was part of the Premiership winning team, before earning a second lease on life when he joined Newcastle Falcons in 2016. He has been capturing points, trophies and the hearts of Falcons' fans ever since. A natural finisher regardless of his age, Goneva has scored more than 50 Premiership tries and was named the league's player of the year for the 2017-18 season.

Semi Radradra's nickname is 'semi-trailer' which tells you all you need to understand the power-based game of this versatile Fijian back. He earned his name because of his attritional style for Parramatta Eels in the Australian National Rugby League competition where he scored 82 tries in 92 outings.

Since his switch to rugby union in 2017, he has played for Toulon and Bordeaux in France and is in the early stage of his international career which could take off at the World Cup. He is a strong, dynamic runner quickly learning the ropes as he showed when he scored a try and was named man of the match when the Barbarians beat England 63-45 at Twickenham in 2018.

Leone Nakarawa is one of the stars of Fijian rugby, both 15-a-side and the sevens game, and a hero in his homeland where he was made an Officer of the Order of Fiji. The 31-year-old is at the peak of his powers and considered by many to be one of the best lock forwards in the world.

He has represented the Flying Fijians more than 50 times since 2009 and won gold with the Fiji sevens team at the 2016 Rio Olympics. Nakarawa ran out for Glasgow Warriors in the Pro14 league and has been with Racing 92 for the last three seasons

239

winning rave reviews. In 2018, he was awarded the European player of the year accolade and is renowned for his athletic approach and ability to off-load the ball in the loose. He will be a major weapon for Fiji in Japan.

Don't overlook: **Lepani Botia**, nicknamed the Demolition Man and now back from a long term injury, and **Viliame Mata**, a wrecking ball of a back row player.

TEAM STYLE

The challenge for Fiji is how to play with more structure in their game, allowing them to build a platform for their irresistible ball carriers and backline. No matter what is said by the team's coaches, Fiji's forwards struggle to compete as a unit with those of Tier 1 nations, and this normally costs them dear.

In the loose, they have a culture of their own, a brand of which they are proud. They take risk-versus-reward rugby to the extreme. At their best they tackle ferociously, smash through static defences, off-load like basketball players and move the ball at pace. It's unique and thrilling to watch.

But when the Flying Fijians are off their game, their tackling lacks discipline and focus, and their passing game verges on suicidal. The error-count goes through the roof, and their wounds are often self-inflicted. Fiji's exuberant, alluring style causes problems for their opponents and themselves in equal measure. Fiji can be mesmeric to watch, but style too often trumps substance.

EXPECTATIONS

Fiji are ranked ninth in the world and have a self-belief – which is not without foundation – that they can overcome any team on their day. Their opening match of Pool D is against an inconsistent Australia who could be the more nervous of the two teams when they lock horns at Sapporo Dome on Saturday, September 21.

Facing the Wallabies this early in the tournament could be perfect for Fiji and a chance to force a shock result. However, it's more likely that Fiji will lose to Australia and Wales, so will be contesting a third-place finish in the pool with Georgia.

The Lelos are ranked 12th in the world and play a style of rugby diametrically opposed to that of the Fijians, making their clash at Hanazono Stadium even more watchable. If any team can be the surprise package of Japan 2019, it is Fiji and, with a rare opportunity to spend quality time together as a unit, it would be unwise to under-estimate this talented, unpredictable squad.

PREDICTION

The dark horses of the tournament, Fiji could fly into the quarter-finals but will more than likely finish third in Pool D.

FIJI'S POOL D FIXTURES

Australia: Saturday, September 21 at Sapporo Dome, ko 1.45pm (GMT 4-45am)

Uruguay: Wednesday, September 25 at Kamaishi Stadium, ko 2.15pm (GMT 5.15am)

Georgia: Thursday, October 3 at Hanazono Stadium, ko 2.15pm (GMT 5.15am)

Wales: Wednesday, October 9 at Oita Stadium, ko 6.45pm (GMT 9.45am)

URUGUAY

FACTS

Nickname: Los Teros
World ranking: 16
Qualification: Americas region play-off winners
World Cup record: P 11, W 2, D 0, L 9
Biggest World Cup win: 27-15 against Spain (1999)
Biggest World Cup defeat: 111-13 by England (2003)
World Cups – 3
Performances: Pool stage – 3

RUGBY WORLD CUP HISTORY

Uruguay are still working on their World Cup history, having only reached the tournament three times and won two matches. Los Teros, named after their country's emblem of the Southern Lapwing bird, have always lived in the shadow of their South American Tier 1 neighbours Argentina, but they have become a solid team in their own right, and reaching Japan 2019 will further enhance their reputation.

Their first World Cup tournament was in 1999 which began with a memorable 27-15 victory over Spain, thanks to tries from Diego Ormaechea, Alfonso Cardoso and Juan Menchaca. They followed this up with a 43-12 setback to Scotland and 39-3 loss to South Africa but were far from disgraced.

They qualified for the 2003 tournament in Australia, but this was a more chastening affair. Uruguay were thumped 72-6 by South Africa, 60-13 by Samoa and 111-13 by eventual champions England, but at least they secured one victory, 24-12 over Georgia with tries from Cardoso, Diego Lamelas and Nicolas Bignoni.

It would be another 12 years before Los Teras reached the World Cup tournament again, this time taking their place in the 2015 competition in England. They were dealt a poor hand being in Pool A – dubbed 'the pool of death' – alongside Australia, Wales, England and Fiji. Unsurprisingly, they failed to win a match and only scored 30 points in their four matches, but it was another page written in their unfolding World Cup story.

Los Teras face Australia, Wales and Fiji again in Japan 2019.

BUILD-UP TO THE 2019 RUGBY WORLD CUP

Los Teros began their run-in to the World Cup by securing qualification in February 2018, overcoming Canada 70-60 in their two-legged Americas region play-off. They won the first leg 38-29 in Vancouver and completed the job in Montevideo winning 32-31, but the nerves were not settled until Andreas Vilaseca scored for the second time late on.

So far, this build-up has taken in a successful defence of the World Rugby Nations Cup and a first-ever win (27-20) against Romania in Bucharest at the end of their November tour of Europe.

Ahead of the 2019 campaign, head coach Esteban Meneses said: "We will have different goals along the season that will help us reach Japan at the top of our game. The Americas Rugby Championship is in February and March, the Sudamerica Six Nations is in May and we'll host the World Rugby Nations Cup again; they will all contribute to make us better every day and arrive in Japan ready."

Uruguay enjoyed a decent Americas Rugby Championship, finishing second in the table to an Argentina XV to whom they lost 35-10. They won their other four matches against Canada 20-17, Chile 20-5, the USA 32-25 and Brazil 42-20.

HEAD COACH

Esteban Meneses has been head coach of Uruguay since 2015 and has led them into a new era of being a Tier 2 nation, having previously been in Tier 3. During the Argentinian's time in charge, Uruguay have enjoyed success in the Americas Championship, South American Championship, South America Cup, Nations Cup and qualified for Rugby World Cup 2019.

Meneses was a former player in Argentina with La Plata, and in Italy with Calvisano and Amatori Alghero before taking up a coaching role with La Plata in 2009. The 47-year-old enjoyed roles at the Buenos Aires Rugby Union and Buenos Aires University club before taking the Uruguay job following a recommendation from Argentina head coach Daniel Hourcade, who was part of the appointment committee.

On being named head coach, Meneses said: "It is a huge challenge and responsibility to be leading a national team. The goal is to grow as a team and work on individual skills that will allow us to play better rugby. Knowing that we will have the support of the Pumas staff was important in my decision and I plan to be in permanent contact with them. Los Teros have great potential and the fact the Uruguayan and Argentine rugby unions are working together is encouraging."

PLAYERS TO WATCH

Juan Manuel Gaminara is nicknamed Garrafa which means gas tank, highlighting the non-stop nature of this consistent Los Teros captain and flanker. Gaminara, 30, plays for Montevideo-based Old Boys and has represented his country since 2010, earning almost 60 caps. Japan will be his second World Cup, but first as captain.

Leandro Leivas is a solid winger who finishes well and who was signed by Canadian team Toronto Arrows for the 2019 Major League Rugby season, one of several Los Teros players who play in this North American professional league.

Leivas, 30, also plays in Uruguay for Old Christians and has scored in excess of 120 points and 24 tries in a little more than 70 appearances for his country. Away from the rugby field, he is a blacksmith and farrier by trade.

Flanker **Diego Magno** is Uruguay's most capped player with more than 80 appearances in the 11 years since making his debut. He was part of the 2015 World Cup squad and a key player as Uruguay qualified for Japan 2019.

A strong back row performer who has scored almost 50 points for Los Teros and who provides leadership on the pitch, 30-year-old Magno was signed by Houston Sabercats in the Major League Rugby competition.

Felipe Berchesi scored 15 points at the 2015 World Cup, half of Uruguay's points in the tournament, and the fly-half remains an integral part of the Los Teros squad. Berchasi plays his club rugby for French side Dax, one of the few Uruguayans to play professional rugby abroad and has racked up more than 30 international appearances since debuting in 2011. The 28-year-old goal kicker played his part in Uruguay finishing second in the Americas Championship in 2019.

Don't overlook: **German Kessler**, a mobile hooker who has scored 40 points for his country, and **Juan Manuel Cat**, a mazy runner at No.10 or No.12.

TEAM STYLE

Given the strong links behind the scenes with Argentina, both formally and informally, it's not surprising that Uruguay mimic many of their senior neighbours' traits in the forwards. A strong scrum and driving game are at the heart of Los Teros rugby, and their challenge will be to find a way around more senior opposition especially when their A-game falls short.

Recently, allies Argentina have played with more expression and Uruguay may attempt to replicate this at times, but don't expect them to veer far away from their comfort zone. They don't have the quality players with elite rugby experience to play anything other than a very structured game.

EXPECTATIONS

Few pundits or seasoned watchers of the game give Uruguay much hope of winning a single match, seeing as they are ranked the weakest team in the group and one of the weakest in the tournament. Not all of their players are professional and few ply their trade outside of Uruguay, and none will have been part of a winning team in a World Cup.

When it comes to talent, experience and history, the odds are against Los Teros. Just being competitive will be a task. In 2015, they conceded 226 points in their four matches. However, many of their squad have performed in this year's professional Major League Rugby competition which will give the players confidence and much needed experience, as head coach Meneses explained.

"It will offer 10 players good competition. Professional rugby, being away from home, being fully focused on the game, which will give them an edge. This will come in handy once we reach Japan."

Los Teros will not lack spirit, commitment or determination, but that might not be enough against the world's best. They might potentially catch Fiji on one of their bad days and have a puncher's chance against Georgia, who may play a similar style, but it would be a surprise if Uruguay were to add to their two victories at the World Cup tournaments.

PREDICTION

Los Teros will be expected to finish last in Pool D and struggle to compete in what is an uncompromising group.

URUGUAY'S FIXTURES IN POOL D

Fiji: Wednesday, September 25 at Kamaishi Stadium, ko 2.15pm
(GMT 5.15am)

Georgia: Sunday, September 29 at Kumagaya Stadium, ko
2.15pm (GMT 5.15am)

Australia: Saturday, October 5 at Oita Stadium, ko 2.15pm
(GMT 5.15am)

Wales: Sunday, October 13 at Kumamoto Stadium, ko 7.15pm
(GMT 8.15am)

CHAPTER 5
EXTRA-TIME

WORLD RANKINGS

The World Rugby rankings give a quick, up-to-date determination of which teams are considered the best in the world at any given time. The rankings are updated every Monday. They are calculated using a points-exchange system, in which sides take points off each other based on the match result. Whatever one side gains, the other loses.

The exchanges are also affected by the relative strength of each team and the margin of victory, there is also an allowance for home advantage. Points exchanges are doubled during the World Cup finals because of the stature of the tournament. All other full international matches are treated the same, in order to be as fair as possible to countries playing a different mix of friendly and competitive matches across the world.

Historically, New Zealand have dominated the standings since they were first used in 2003, while Australia and England have also topped the table for periods, especially after their respective World Cup wins. Ireland had been pushing to overtake New Zealand at the top of the rankings, having enjoyed a memorable 2018. However, a below par Six Nations championship saw them slip back to third place in the list. Wales have moved up to second in the rankings, having won the Six Nations, while outside of the Tier 1 teams, Georgia, Hong Kong and the Netherlands have also moved in the right direction.

Nine of the top 10 rankings are held by Tier 1 teams, the only exception being Fiji who are in ninth place. The solitary Tier 1 team outside the top 10 is Italy in 14th place.

Top 30 world rankings (on April 15, 2019):

1. New Zealand
2. Wales
3. Ireland
4. England
5. South Africa
6. Australia
7. Scotland
8. France
9. Fiji
10. Argentina
11. Japan
12. Georgia
13. Tonga
14. Italy
15. USA
16. Uruguay
17. Samoa
18. Romania
19. Spain
20. Russia
21. Canada

22. Namibia

23. Portugal

24. Brazil

25. Hong Kong

26. Netherlands

27. Belgium

28. Germany

29. Chile

30. Korea

(There are 105 world ranked teams in total.)

RUGBY TIERS

World Rugby, the sport's international governing body, classifies countries into three tiers: 1, 2 and 3.

Tier 1 (10 teams): England, France, Ireland, Italy, Scotland, Wales, Argentina, Australia, New Zealand, South Africa.

These teams are the most senior in the world game, funded accordingly by World Rugby, and play in Tier 1 tournaments; the Northern Hemisphere teams in the Six Nations and the Southern Hemisphere teams in the Rugby Championship.

Tier 2 (13 teams): Georgia, Portugal, Romania, Russia, Spain, Canada, USA, Uruguay, Namibia, Japan, Fiji, Samoa and Tonga.

The 13 Tier 2 teams are those most likely to achieve Tier 1 status in the foreseeable future; Argentina and Italy being the two teams to make that big jump in the last two decades. Fiji, Georgia and Japan are considered the strongest of this tier of teams and perhaps most likely to make that step up next.

Tier 2 teams receive funding by World Rugby to help them achieve that aim. Fiji, Samoa and Japan have earned notable successes in the Rugby World Cup over the years and now Japan are hosting this year's tournament – a first for a Tier 2 nation.

Tier 2 teams from Pacific countries participate in the World Rugby Pacific Nations Cup, the European countries play in the Rugby Europe Championships, the North and South American teams take part in the Americas Rugby Championship, while the Asian teams meet in the Asia Rugby Championship. These regional tournaments are often sub-divided into divisions based on ability and ranking.

Tier 3 teams: There are currently 110 Tier 3 teams which are in the process of developing the sport in their country. Most are countries where rugby is not traditionally played, or have small populations making growth in the sport a challenge.

Nine are known as Development 1 teams and are the strongest Tier 3 teams. They are: Belgium, Germany, Brazil, Chile, Ivory Coast, Kenya, Zimbabwe, Hong Kong and Korea.

The other 101 teams are known as Development 2 teams.

WORLD RUGBY

World Rugby is the world governing body for rugby union and comprised of up to 123 member or associate member unions from around the globe.

From its offices in Dublin, World Rugby organises and authorises numerous competitions in the six rugby regions around the world (Africa, Asia, Europe, North America, South America and Oceania), junior worldwide events, the World Rugby Sevens Series and, most importantly, the Rugby World Cup every four years. It also organises the women's game and the Women's Rugby World Cup every four years, the last one being held in Northern Ireland and the Republic of Ireland in 2017.

Originally named the International Rugby Football Board (IRFB), the body was formed in 1886 by Ireland, Scotland and Wales and, fours year later, welcomed England on board. Australia, New Zealand and South Africa were accepted as full members in 1949 and France in 1978. A further 80 countries joined as members between 1987 and 1999. The body was renamed the International Rugby Board (IRB) in 1998 and World Rugby in 2014.

The World Rugby Council meets twice a year and manages and controls the affairs of World Rugby. It is the supreme legislative authority of World Rugby. It oversees World Rugby's strategic plan, application of policy decisions and selects the host nation(s) for the Rugby World Cup.

The Council considers recommendations of the General Assembly. A General Assembly of the full membership is convened every two years and may make recommendations to the Council, and may consider business that the Council has referred to it. However, the General Assembly has no legislative powers.

The Executive Committee ensures the management and operation of World Rugby. It formulates and monitors the implementation of the World Rugby's strategic plan, business plan, operational plan, and budget. Former England captain Sir Bill Beaumont was elected World Rugby chairman on July 1, 2016, taking over the reins from Frenchman Bernard Lapasset.

World Rugby's core objective is to grow the game in such a way that it maintains the sport's stated core values of integrity, passion, solidarity, discipline and respect. The body also aims to improve the popularity of the sport, expand its worldwide image and generate funds to support its objectives and member unions.

World Rugby achieved a long-held dream when sevens rugby was admitted into Olympics at Rio 2016. The competition, memorably won by Fiji, was a success, exposing rugby to a massive worldwide television audience. However, the World Cup is the biggest driver of publicity and revenue in the sport, and World Rugby is currently financially dependent upon its success.

World Cup revenue usually comes from different sources such as gate receipts, broadcasting rights, sponsorship and other rights, and a fee paid by the tournament hosts. The home union keeps the revenue from gate receipts while World Rugby normally takes the income from broadcasting rights, sponsorship and tournament fee. Australia paid £35 million to host the 2003 tournament while France paid £50 million four years later, New Zealand £55 million in 2011, and £80 million was paid by England in 2015. To host the 2023 World Cup, France are believed to have paid approximately £120 million as a tournament fee.

The 2007 Rugby World Cup helped World Rugby to make a surplus of £122 million and, from 2005-12, £79 million was invested in supporting Tier 2 nations.

Ahead of the 2019 Rugby World Cup, World Rugby has stated: "The global rugby community comprises 9.1 million players and 338 million fans affiliated via 123 national member unions in six regions and driven by the commercial success of Rugby World Cup. World Rugby is investing £482 million at all levels of the game between 2016 and 2019, eclipsing the previous four-year cycle by 38 percent, to ensure strong and sustainable growth."

In return for awarding the 2023 Rugby World Cup hosting rights to France, World Rugby is expected to reach net revenues in excess of £400 million.

Over the years, World Rugby has overseen, or sometimes created, controversy in the game whether it was their hotly disputed decision to award France the 2023 World Cup, the inability to streamline international player eligibility rules or the handling of disciplinary matters.

In February 2019, World Rugby's proposal to hold a world league every year – except in World Cup year – featuring the unions from the Six Nations and Rugby Championship competitions plus Japan and Fiji was widely criticised as money-grabbing, devaluing the World Cup and not being considerate of players' well-being. World Rugby has refuted these suggestions.

World Rugby has published and maintained the World Rugby rankings of men's national teams since 2003 and hosts the high-profile annual World Rugby Awards.

WORLD RUGBY AWARDS 2018

Ireland fly-half **Johnny Sexton** was named World Player of the Year in November 2018 at the sport's glitzy annual awards ceremony in Monte Carlo. It's the highest accolade that can be awarded to a player and ended six consecutive years when the award was won by a New Zealander.

Sexton – who described winning the award as 'an incredible honour' – beat off competition from four other nominees: All Blacks Beauden Barrett and Rieko Loane, and Springboks Faf de Klerk and Malcolm Marx.

Given their impressive record in the previous 12 months – including winning the Six Nations Championship with a Grand Slam and beating New Zealand for a second time in two years – it was no surprise that **Ireland** were named World Rugby Team of the Year, and that their coach **Joe Schmidt** was Coach of the Year.

France's **Jordan Joseph** was Junior Player of the Year, while New Zealand's **Brodie Retallick** won the Try of the Year award for his effort against Australia in Sydney in August 2018.

The panels for the 2019 World Rugby Awards have been announced.

Former Samoa centre Seilala Mapusua, Ireland captain Fiona Coghlan and two-time Women's Rugby World Cup winner Melodie Robinson of New Zealand will come onto the Men's 15s panel to join a blend of test stars and World Rugby Hall of Fame inductees in Maggie Alphonsi, Fabien Galthié, George Gregan, Richie McCaw, Brian O'Driscoll, Agustín Pichot and John Smit.

Two Rugby World Cup winners in former New Zealand captain Fiao'o Faamausili and Springbok Bryan Habana join Felipe Contepomi and Jamie Heaslip on the panel for the Breakthrough Player of the Year.

The panel of Alphonsi, O'Driscoll, Pichot, Rugby World Cup 2003 winning coach Clive Woodward and former South Africa and Italy coach Nick Mallett will determine the World Rugby Coach and Team of the Year.

The ceremony will take place at The Prince Park Tower Tokyo on Sunday, November 3 – the day after the World Cup final.

HOW WE WON THE RUGBY WORLD CUP

Famous Rugby World Cup winners recall their time at the tournament and what it took to lift the Webb Ellis Cup.

1987 – DAVID KIRK (NEW ZEALAND)

All Blacks captain David Kirk led his team to a 29-9 success over France in the first Rugby World Cup final played at Eden Park, Auckland. He told The Guardian newspaper in 2003 that the key to winning was 'pressure and defence.' He added: "The French had running forwards and a strong midfield. But our midfield made tackles on the gain line and the tries came for us after that." He said that the quarter-final against Scotland, which the All Blacks won 30-3, was the toughest match because: "The thought of losing a quarter-final at home was emotionally stressful."

Scrum-half Kirk also explained the game plan which was ultimately successful. "The forwards were to be aggressive with the powerful loose-running back row of Wayne 'Buck' Shelford, Michael Jones and Alan Whetton working with me."

1991 – NICK FARR-JONES (AUSTRALIA)

Nick Farr-Jones was captain of the Wallabies when they lifted the Webb Ellis Cup, having narrowly beaten hosts England 12-6 in the final at Twickenham, a match the Aussie skipper admitted was their toughest of the competition.

The scrum-half said the team built their success on 'getting things right' and 'minimising errors.' He added: "It was about concentrating on your game and trusting those around you. I would like to think (winning the final) was because of our great attacking play, but we didn't win 50 percent of possession. Our desperation in defence won it for us."

1995 – FRANCOIS PIENNAR (SOUTH AFRICA)

Captain and open side flanker Francois Piennar had the joy of winning the World Cup on home soil when the Springboks beat the All Blacks 15-12 after extra-time, in an historic final at Ellis Park in Johannesburg.

Piennar, who memorably received the Webb Ellis Cup from South African president Nelson Mandela, has said that discipline was the key factor in his team's success in the final. He said: "We had to keep our heads at all times. We scored a try that was not given, and it would have been easy to lose our cool."

Piennar admitted that the biggest challenge the team, and he as captain, faced was in the pool stage. He said the key was: "Refocusing after our hooker James Dalton and wing Pieter Hendriks were sent off for fighting in the game against Canada."

1999 – JOHN EALES (AUSTRALIA)

Wallabies captain John Eales guided his team to World Cup glory in 1999, beating France 35-12 in the final at the Millennium Stadium in Cardiff. The lock, who was capped 86 times by his country, believes initially being based in the Irish countryside helped them remain focused.

"Being in the backblocks of Dublin, we were able to prepare out of the limelight," he said in an interview with The Guardian newspaper in 2003, adding: "It enabled us to concentrate solely on what we needed to do."

He added that the biggest test came in the final 'because of what was going on' (a reference to eye-gouging allegations by the Wallabies about France). Eales also highlighted other reasons for success including his team's defence and their ability to 'get the basics right'.

2003 – WILL GREENWOOD (ENGLAND)

Centre Will Greenwod scored five tries for England in the 2003 tournament as they became the first and, to date, only Northern Hemisphere team to lift the Webb Ellis Cup.

The tense 20-17 victory over hosts Australia in the final will always be remembered for Jonny Wilkinson's match-winning drop goal in the last minute of extra-time. The result could have gone either way, but Greenwood believes England were destined to win.

"It's tough to think there's ever been a better England team before or after. It was a special time," he said. "We won it because we were a better team, which meant we were able to control emotions, go behind, not score a point in the second half to finish 17-17 in an Olympic stadium which wasn't ours, and still believe we wouldn't lose. We knew each other inside out. The best team doesn't always win, but I felt the best team won that night."

2007 – JOHN SMIT (SOUTH AFRICA)

John Smit has described winning the tense 2007 Rugby World Cup final 15-6 against England in Paris as a 'dream come true'.

The Springboks captain said: "The guys were nervous in the build up to the final, we knew it would not be another 36-0 encounter (the score that South Africa had beaten England by in the pool stage). Beforehand we said that, we had one hand on the cup by winning well in the semi-final, and the only way to win it was to play as if it was your last test, the only one that had mattered in your life. We did that. We played within ourselves because we were so nervous. Tactically it was astute, but we could have taken more risks to find holes and space. We did what was required to win. It was tight but we felt in control."

Smit added: "When the final whistle went, I fell to the ground, tears were rolling down my face and then I got up and hugged the referee because he was the nearest person to me!"

2011 – STEPHEN DONALD (NEW ZEALAND)

Fourth choice fly-half Stephan Donald played his part in the All Blacks' 8-7 victory over France in a tense and ferocious final in Auckland in 2011. Called into the squad, following injuries to Dan Carter and Colin Slade, Donald came on as a replacement for the Aaron Cruden, who was injured during the match, and kicked the winning points.

"I craved to be out there and craved the opportunity," he said, but when France scored a try to make it 8-7 and had the momentum, Donald recalled: "It was pretty sickening at the time. But looking back, it's all something to be proud of. The boys kept fronting up for the whole second half, tackle after tackle. It was an amazing time."

2015 – RICHIE MCCAW (NEW ZEALAND)

New Zealand fly-half Dan Carter was the man of the match, as the All Blacks became the first team to claim back-to-back Rugby World Cup titles beating Australia 34-17 at Twickenham. Captain Richie McCaw said they had focused on retaining their title and creating history.

"We said four years ago that we get on the road again with this being the end goal, and try and do something no one else has done," he said. "I'm so proud of the guys. We lost a bit of momentum in the second half, but we kept our composure and came back strong."

McCaw added that his team's experience pulled them through when the Wallabies came back. He said: "I knew the momentum was against us, but we've been in those situations before. It's a matter of not panicking. I've done it many times over the years, but to do it in a World Cup final shows the calibre of men we've got."

THREATS TO THE 2019 RUGBY WORLD CUP

Never has a World Cup been played in a country where the possibility of a natural disaster been so real and life-threatening. Japan has a history of suffering earthquakes, tsunamis and typhoons, and in the month of September, when the World Cup begins, the threat is at its height. In June 2018, there was an earthquake in Osaka and the following month saw flash flooding and a heatwave in which many people died. In September, Japan suffered its biggest typhoon for a generation. The flooding and tidal surges in the west of the country killed at least 11 people, injuring dozens more.

Shortly after, a 6.7 magnitude earthquake in the north started landslides which killed 39 people, including in Sapporo where England will face Tonga on Sunday, September 22.

Speaking exactly a year before the competition begins, Rugby World Cup 2019 tournament director Alan Gilpin said contingency plans had been drawn up for any natural disasters which may hit Japan.

"It's a real hot topic for us right now. Teams will be arriving next year at a time when Japan has experienced a pretty significant typhoon and earthquake," he said.

"We are planning right through, from what happens if a team hotel or training venue is lost, to what happens if one or more match venues are lost. We are working through all these scenarios.

"It's a complex piece and something that we would do for every tournament, but this one has a heightened sense of realism to it. We have to take it seriously. But there's also a heightened sense of comfort that Japan deals with these issues all the time. It's not as though we're dealing with a one-off here. As they very calmly tell us, they have 480 earthquakes a year."

Being positive, Gilpin said Japan knows how to deal with such issues.

"Japan copes very well with the adverse weather and other environmental issues they have," he said. "Their venues and hotels are built to withstand incredibly adverse conditions, so in some respects they are less affected. What you tend to see in Japan is older buildings and structures being affected when they have either earthquakes or typhoons, but we obviously have to take that seriously."

He added that it would be 'unprecedented' for a natural disaster to affect the whole country.

In an interview in January 2019, Gilpin stressed: "It would appear that it's that first period of the tournament — when it is still typhoon season — that we're likely to have some issues. "That is the busiest part of the tournament, so we've got to be ready."

Gilpin suggested that if the elements do affect the tournament, then knock-out matches could be postponed but any pool matches, because of the tight schedule, might have to be voided and declared draws.

Aside from the threat of terrorism, which is always a concern at a huge global event, one of the lesser, but more unique, challenges for organisers is players with tattoos. The Japanese public tend to associate tattoos with members of organised crime, the Yakuza. Many players of other nations have visible tattoos, particularly those of Pacific Island descent.

Gilpin said that the tournament organisers were working to dispel the fears that the public might have. "We will make the public aware that people with tattoos in a World Cup context are not part of the Yakuza. That's where the issue comes from," he said.

"We have done a lot in the last year or so with the teams to get them to understand that. They want to respect the Japanese culture so will buy into the idea of putting a rash-vest on in the pool, or in a gym. We'll position it as self-policing."

ON THE LIGHTER SIDE

International rugby is a serious game and the World Cup its pinnacle, but that doesn't mean there aren't some light-hearted moments to be found.

Here are 10 rugby jokes and quips to make you smile.

1. Told by an Australian in 2011: Head coach Martin Johnson takes the England team out for training and tells everyone to assume their normal position.

So they all go and stand behind the goal posts and wait for the conversion.

2. Talking about the imposing figure of New Zealand ace Jonah Lomu in 2011, former All Blacks great Colin Meads said: "I've seen a lot of people like him, but they weren't on the wing."

3. A message sent to the New Zealand team before the 1995 World Cup semi-final read: "Remember that rugby is a team game; all 14 of you, make sure you pass the ball to Jonah Lomu."

4. Before professional rugby was legitimised, former Australian winger and World Cup winner David Campese, speaking in 1991, said: "I'm still an amateur, of course, but I became a millionaire five years ago."

5. Told by a New Zealander before 2003: Question – What do you call an Englishman with the Rugby World Cup in his hands?

Answer: The engraver.

6. Two Tongans, two Fijians and a Samoan walk into a bar, the barman says: "Congratulations on your selection for the New Zealand Rugby World Cup squad."

7. England rugby fan to a Scotland fan: "There's a fine line between success and failure in international rugby; it's called Hadrian's Wall."

8. Question: What is the greatest World Cup tournament in French rugby history?

Answer: The next one.

9. A player comes off the pitch and tells the medic "When I touch my legs, arms, stomach, everywhere, it really hurts. What's the problem?"

The medic replies: "You've broken your finger."

10. Question: What's the difference between Scotland at the World Cup, and a tea bag?

Answer: The tea bag stays in the cup longer.

CHAPTER 6
THE DECADE AHEAD

RUGBY WORLD CUP 2023 IN FRANCE

The next World Cup in four years is scheduled to be hosted by France after they were controversially chosen ahead of main rivals South Africa and Ireland.

An independent evaluation by a World Rugby committee on the merits of three remaining bids – after the USA, Argentina and Italy withdrew or declined to bid – came down in favour of South Africa, with France in second place and Ireland third. The report marked each bid based on commercial success, venues and host cities, tournament infrastructure, vision and hosting concept, and organisation and schedule.

But ignoring the recommendations of the public report, the World Rugby Council voted in a secret ballot and, in round one, France gained 18 votes, South Africa 13 and Ireland 8. With Ireland eliminated for the second round, a new vote saw France pick up 24 votes to South Africa's 15, amid much acrimony.

The key factor in favour of France winning the rights seems to have been their guarantee of a net revenue of £350 million to

World Rugby, some £80 million more than those of their two rivals. So, France – in the year of the 200th anniversary of the sport's founding by William Webb Ellis – will solely host the tournament, using nine different venues from September 8 to October 21. The final of this tenth Rugby World Cup will be played at the Stade de France in Paris.

The 2023 tournament may welcome more teams than ever before as there are discussions about increasing numbers from the current 20 to 24. As is now the case, it is expected that a maximum of 13 teams will qualify automatically for the tournament; the top three teams in each of the four pools at the 2019 World Cup, plus the 2023 hosts (France). The successful teams following regional tournaments in Africa, Asia, Europe, Oceania, North America and South America will also be added to these.

The game's governing body, World Rugby, is keen to grow the sport in new markets which will boost revenues, popularity and participation. The sport is becoming increasingly mainstream in some countries – especially Hong Kong, USA, Russia, Spain, Brazil and Germany – and these are seen by World Rugby as potential areas of growth.

The expansion of the World Cup is seen as the obvious way of reaching countries which were previously rugby outposts. If the decision to expand the number of nations is not made for the 2023 tournament, World Rugby has said that expansion is still its objective at some point in the future, perhaps in 2027.

RUGBY WORLD CUP 2023 VENUES

Stade de France (Paris), capacity 80,698

Stade Velodrome (Marseille), capacity 67,394

Parc Olympique Lyonnais (Lyon), capacity 59,186

Stade Pierre-Mauroy (Lille), capacity 50,157

Matmut Atlantique (Bordeaux), capacity 42,115

Stade Geoffroy-Guichard (Saint-Etienne), capacity 41,965

Allianz Riviera (Nice), capacity 35,624

Stade de la Beaujoire (Nantes), capacity 35,322

Stadium de Toulouse (Toulouse), capacity 33,150

THE FUTURE OF THE RUGBY WORLD CUP

The Rugby World Cup's future, and the importance it plays in the perception and finances of the worldwide game, is assured – for now. No-one doubts the need for a tournament every four years and, indeed, World Rugby and the individual national governing bodies, are financially dependent on its growth and success. Hence, the likelihood is that the tournament will soon expand from 20 nations to at least 24 nations.

South Africa will no doubt throw their hat into the ring to host the 2027 tournament, especially after controversially losing out on the 2023 event to France, as will Australia. And with three consecutive tournaments having been awarded to Northern Hemisphere countries (England 2015, Japan 2019 and France 2023), a return to the Southern Hemisphere for 2027 seems to be favoured. Whether that means returning to South Africa or Australia or taking the competition to new markets such as

Argentina – who showed interest in the 2023 bid process – remains to be seen.

USA Rugby were also briefly interested in hosting the 2023 event, and an offer by them in the future would have to be seriously considered because of the undoubted increased profile that would bring to the game.

World Rugby chairman Sir Bill Beaumont was open in his assessment of the future of the tournament. In 2018, he said that World Rugby 'will have to have a philosophical debate going forward' over where future World Cups should be held. He added: "It's important that we are commercially successful, but we do need to have that debate whether the next World Cup following France will go to an emerging country, or an established country that actually needs a bit of help as well."

Ultimately the revenue which the World Cup can generate for the sport is the deciding factor, meaning many smaller nations may never host the tournament or, at least, be forced to co-host with one or more partners. Yet the performance of these emerging nations will strongly influence the growth of the tournament, as the gap shrinks between them and the traditional giants of rugby.

Recent performances at World Cups by Argentina, Fiji, Samoa, Japan and Georgia proves what can be achieved. Beaumont agreed that there is more competition in the tournament now, and highlighted Fiji as an example of a Tier 2 team which could perform well in Japan.

He said that 'none of the so-called fancied teams will want to play against Fiji' who have twice upset the odds to reach the quarter-finals. "Last World Cup, they (Fiji) had a very tough group," he added. "This time, if they get their act together, they could really get to the quarter-finals or even go further."

Beaumont may have been using this as a way of promoting the tournament to a wider audience, while throwing a bone to a Tier 2 audience which is often critical of World Rugby, but it is true that World Cup tournaments are more competitive than ever and certainly from when it began in 1987.

It is also fundamental to the global appeal of the tournament, and the sport, that more nations are encouraged to raise their game and compete on a more level playing field. The financial success of the Rugby World Cup is an integral part of this objective. World Rugby also knows that there is an increasing number of challenges to the tournament from outside the game, as more sports look to grab a slice of the global sporting market.

Dealing with more competition on one hand and the varying concerns of its member unions on the other – while maintaining the Rugby World Cup's position as the third biggest sporting tournament on the planet – will increasingly be the defining challenge for World Rugby in the years to come.

RUGBY SEVENS AND THE OLYMPICS

There is no denying the positive impact sevens has made on rugby as a whole; driving the image of rugby – both sevens and 15-a-side – to a wider audience. Some new players and spectators – whether paying to watch a game or viewing on television or the internet – may just confine themselves to sevens, but others may be drawn into the 15-a-side game, or even dabble in both.

Either way, sevens is a gateway to the sport as a whole and its inclusion in the 2016 Olympics in Rio has already helped create huge interest which World Rugby is desperate to build on. It is believed that the impact of sevens in Rio, and the upcoming 2020 Games in Tokyo, will play a bigger role in promoting the sport than even the Rugby World Cup.

The popularity of rugby was already growing around the world, which gave the sport the opportunity to apply for Olympic status. To qualify for the Olympics, sports must be played competitively in at least 75 countries on four continents and be included in numerous regional multi-sports tournaments – like the Commonwealth Games. Rugby was already on the move, but there is no doubt that the Olympics has been transformational. More countries are taking the sport seriously with funding and governmental support increasing.

NEW NATIONS

Expect more nations to grow their game as funding from World Rugby and exposure through the Rugby World Cup and the Olympics are set to continue. The USA, China, Brazil and Germany are seen as areas of real growth for all forms of the game within the next decade.

NEW PLAYERS

There are currently seven million rugby players in the world, combining all forms of the game, and predicted to rise to 10 million by the end of the decade, and to 15 million by 2026.

The women's game is growing quickly in both developed and developing rugby markets, with some predictions suggesting half a million players per year. By 2026, a total of 40 percent of rugby players will be female.

At a professional level, players from rugby league are expected to move into the sevens game in increasing numbers as the Olympic sport becomes better funded. The primary skills of rugby league players – tackling man and ball, speed and ball handling – are directly transferable to sevens.

NEW AUDIENCES

By 2026, rugby, like most sports, will be consumed by younger generations and new viewers more often through social platforms and using devices other than televisions. Sevens will lead a transformed television viewing experience demonstrating the speed, skill and athleticism of players through on-player cameras, virtual reality cameras and digital packages that will help connect the sport to new audiences.

OVERVIEW

A report from The Futures Company, commissioned by HSBC, ahead of the 2016 Olympics concluded that in the next decade 'it seems entirely possible' that:

- Countries with little rugby tradition will be internationally competitive, certainly at sevens

- The overall number of players—and the proportion of female players—will have doubled

- The higher profile of sevens will create new national competitions between clubs or franchises

- Sevens will emerge as a summer sport in its own right

- Audiences will have changed and will connect with the sport in new ways. Younger people will find the game through social platforms rather than traditional media. Meanwhile, innovations that capture the speed and power of the game will transform TV coverage.

GLOSSARY

An explanation of terms and phrases used in this guidebook or what you might hear or read by following the Rugby World Cup.

Advantage Line: Imaginary line that extends across the field from where the last scrum, ruck, maul, lineout or play of the ball was formed. This is used as a measure of how much ground a team has gained or lost. Also known as the gain line.

Africa Cup: The annual tournament involving African nations, excluding South Africa - the continent's only Tier 1 nation.

All Blacks: Nickname of the New Zealand rugby team.

Asia Rugby Championship: The annual tournament involving Asian nations.

Against the head: Rare occurrence of the ball being lost in the scrum by the attacking team which has the put-in.

Americas Rugby Championship: Annual tournament involving an Argentina XV (not their 1st XV), Brazil, Canada, Chile, USA and Uruguay.

Azzurri: Nickname of the Italian rugby team.

Back row: Collective name for the three players at the back of the scrum – the two flankers and the No.8.

Backs: Group of players normally numbered from No.9 to No.15 who do not participate in the scrums or lineouts, except for the scrum-half (No.9). They tend to be quicker and more agile than the forwards. Also known as the backline.

Bears: Nickname of the Russian rugby team.

Binding: The careful method players use to grip each other to form a secure and safe scrum, ruck or maul.

Bledisloe Cup: Three matches played in a year between Australia and New Zealand, two of the matches being part of the Rugby Championship.

Blindside: The narrow side of the pitch in relation to a scrum or a breakdown in play. Also known as the short side or weak side.

Blitz Defence: When the whole defensive line moves forward quickly as a unit, and when the ball leaves the ruck or maul to prevent the attacking team gaining ground, ideally tackling them behind the advantage line.

Blood Bin: A bleeding player must leave the pitch for medical attention and can be temporarily replaced by a substitute. The bleeding player must be permanently replaced if away from the pitch for more than 15 minutes.

Bomb: Ball kicked high in the air, chased by the attacking team, aimed at putting pressure on the opposition's fullback

Box kick: A high, over-the-shoulder kick, used mostly by scrum-halves, in tight attacking or defensive situations.

Brave Blossoms: Nickname of the Japanese rugby team.

Breakdown: The short period of play just after the tackle, and before and during the ruck. The breakdown has developed as a point of competition for the ball and is a vital facet of the game that both teams normally attempt to dominate.

Calcutta Cup: Annual match between England and Scotland, part of the Six Nations Championship, which has been played for since 1879. The cup is made from the coins remaining after the Calcutta Rugby Club disbanded in the 1920s.

Canucks: Nickname of the Canadian rugby team.

Cap: Every time a player plays for a team they are technically, although not actually, awarded a cap and the term is used to calculate the number of appearances a player makes for that team.

Centre: Name given to either of the backs wearing the No.12 (inside centre) or No.13 (outside centre) jerseys. Also collectively known as the midfield. The inside centre is also known as second five-eighths in Australia and New Zealand.

Charge Down: The blocking of a kick by an opposition player.

Collapsing the Scrum: When the scrum goes to ground or collapses. Often used as an illegal, spoiling tactic.

Conversion: The kick at the posts after the awarding of a try. A successful conversion between the posts earns two points.

Dot down: The informal term for the act of touching the ball on the ground, on or past the try line, to score a try.

Drop Goal: A kick at the posts taken at any time a team is close to the opposition's try line. A successful kick between the posts is worth three points, but the ball must hit the ground first before being kicked.

Eagles: Nickname of the USA rugby team.

Fend: A player pushes away a would-be tackler with the palm of their hand on an outstretched arm, while having the ball securely held in the other arm. Also known as a hand-off.

Flanker: Either of the two forwards wearing the No.6 or No.7 jerseys. They tend to be mobile but powerful, hunting down opponents to win possession and make ground, or set up an attack. Also known as a wing forward.

Fly-Half: The back wearing of the No.10 jersey, who receives the ball from the scrum-half and is often the pivotal playmaker of the team. Also known as stand-off, outside-half or first five-eighths.

Flying Fijians: Nickname of the Fijian rugby team.

Forward Pass: An illegal pass to a player who is ahead of the ball.

Forwards: The group of players numbered No.1 to No.8 who bind together in the scrum, most rucks and mauls, and who line up for a lineout. They are traditionally bigger and stronger than backs, but not as mobile.

Free-Kick: A kick awarded to a team for a minor infringement of the laws. It cannot be taken directly at the posts except by a drop goal.

Front Row: The name for the prop-hooker-prop combination at the front of a scrum.

Fullback: The back wearing the No.15 jersey who normally plays deep behind the backline from where he can collect high kicks, be the last line of defence, or instigate counter-attacks.

Grand Slam: A Six Nations Championship won by a team that has been victorious in all five matches.

Grubber: A low kick which causes the ball to bounce and roll along the ground.

Haka: A Maori war dance performed by the New Zealand rugby team before each of their international matches.

Half-Backs: The common collective name used in the Northern Hemisphere for the scrum-half and fly-half combination.

Head Injury Assessment (HIA): A series of tests used in professional rugby to determine whether a player is suffering from concussion. The player must leave the field to receive the assessment but can return if given the all-clear by medical staff.

Heads-up rugby: When a player (or team) is alert and reacts to the live situation they face, not simply sticking rigidly to a set plan.

High Tackle: A dangerous and illegal tackle above the line of the shoulders.

Home Nations: England, Ireland, Scotland and Wales.

Hooker: The front row forward wearing the No.2 jersey whose role is to win the ball in the scrum from his team's put-in, or block the opposition when they have the put-in. The hooker also normally throws the ball in at the lineout.

Ikale Tahi: Nickname of the Tongan rugby team.

Knock On: Losing, dropping or knocking the ball forward from a player's hand. This results in the ball being awarded to the other team in a scrum. Also known as a knock forward.

Lelos: Nickname of the Georgian rugby team.

Les Bleus: Nickname of the French rugby team.

Lineout: The set-play restarting the game after the ball has been taken out of the playing area or kicked into touch. The throw must be directly down the middle of the two lines.

Lock: Either of the forwards usually wearing the No.4 or No.5 jerseys. Traditionally the tallest and most powerful players on the pitch, their main function is to add power to the scrum and catch the ball at lineouts.

Loose: When the ball is in open play, not part of a set-play like a scrum or a lineout.

Loose Head: The prop in a scrum wearing the No.1 jersey, named because his head is outside the opposition tight-head prop's shoulders. Part of their role is to disrupt the scrum when the other team has the put-in.

Loose Forwards: Common name for the flankers and No.8.

Los Pumas: Nickname of the Argentinian rugby team.

Los Teros: Nickname of the Uruguayan rugby team.

Major League Rugby (MLR): A professional rugby union competition and the top-level championship for clubs in North America. In the 2019 season, it was contested by eight teams from the USA and one from Canada.

Manu Samoa: Nickname of the Samoan rugby team.

Maul: A maul is typically called by the referee after a runner has come into contact and the ball is still being held by a player, and once any combination of at least three players have bound themselves. The main difference from a ruck, which is similar to a maul, is that the ball is not on the ground. A maul is a way of controlling the ball and moving towards the opposition try line in a straight line (driving maul), or by changing the point of attack (rolling maul).

Midfield: The collective name for the inside and outside centres together, and also the middle area of the rugby pitch (which is where the centres are most often found).

No.8: The forward who wears the No.8 jersey and is at the base of the scrum, controlling the movement of the scrum and deciding when and if the ball is released to the scrum-half.

Oceania Rugby: The regional governing body for rugby union in Oceania which has 14 full members including Australia, Fiji, New Zealand, Samoa and Tonga.

Offsides: Different phases of the game have their own offside laws. During rucks, scrums, lineouts and mauls, an imaginary line across the pitch is present and any player crossing the line before the set piece is completed is offside. The offence is penalised with a penalty kick.

Openside: The wide side of the pitch in relation to a scrum or a breakdown in play.

Pacific Nations Cup: The annual competition, organised by Oceania Rugby, between Fiji, Samoa, Tonga and, on occasions, invited teams. Canada, Japan and the USA took part in the 2019 tournament.

Pack: Another term for the forwards, usually when they are bound for a scrum.

Penalty Kick: An uncontested kick awarded to a team for a major infringement of the laws by the other team. It can be kicked at the posts for three points, if successful, or kicked into touch to earn territory and likely retain possession from a lineout.

Penalty Try: The awarding of a try and conversion (seven points) due to a flagrant violation by an opposing team that prevents an obvious try from being scored.

Prop: Either of the forwards wearing the No.1 jersey (loose head prop) or No.3 jersey (tight head prop). Their main responsibilities are to support the hooker during scrums and the second rows during the lineout.

Premiership: The top level of professional club rugby in England made up of 12 teams.

Pro14: The top flight professional club competition involving 14 teams in total from Ireland (4), Italy (2), Scotland (2), South Africa (2) and Wales (4).

Pushover Try: A try scored by the forward pack as a unit in a scrum or ruck by pushing the opposition backwards across the try line from where an attacking player, often the No.8, can touch the ball down.

Restart: The kick restarting play after a half or after points are scored.

Ruck: Typically called by the referee after a runner has come into contact and the ball is grounded, and once any combination of at least three players have bound themselves. The primary difference between a ruck and a maul is that in a ruck, the ball is on the ground.

Rugby Championship: A competition contested annually by Argentina, Australia, New Zealand and South Africa. Before Argentina joined in the 2012 tournament, it was known as the Tri Nations.

Rugby Europe Championship: The championships for Tier 2 and Tier 3 European nations split into six groups (Championship – often known as Six Nations B, Trophy and four regional conferences).

Rugby League: A 13-a-side form of rugby which originated in Northern England and split from Rugby Union in 1895, developing its own laws. Its next World Cups - for both men and women - take place in England in 2021.

Rugby Union: A 15-a-side form of rugby, thought to have been conceived in 1823 at Rugby School in England, is administered globally by World Rugby. It has a men's World Cup in Japan in 2019 and a Women's World Cup in New Zealand in 2021.

Rugger: Informal name for rugby.

RWC: Abbreviation of the Rugby World Cup.

Scrum: The set-play for restarting the game after a knock-on or forward pass. The forwards from each side bind together and then the two packs come together to allow the scrum-half with the put-in to deliver the ball into the scrum.

Scrum-Half: The back wearing the No.9 jersey, who normally feeds the ball into a scrum and retrieves the ball at the base of scrums, rucks and mauls. Also known as a half-back.

Second Row: Collective name for the two locks in the forward pack.

Sent off: A player is ordered off the pitch for the remainder of the match by the referee, who usually shows a red card, for serious foul play, violent conduct or two cautionable offences.

Sevens: A seven-a-side variant of Rugby Union which is non-stop, fast and played over two seven-minute halves. Popular at all levels with men and women, the game is organised globally by World Rugby, has an annual world series and a World Cup every four years – the last one being in San Francisco in 2018. It has been an Olympic sport since 2016.

Sin Bin: A player is sent to the sin bin for 10 minutes when shown a yellow card by the referee for a cautionable offence.

Sipi Tau: A war dance performed by the Tongan rugby team before each of their international matches.

Siva Tau: A war dance performed by the Samoan rugby team before each of their international matches.

Six Nations Championship: The annual Tier 1 competition played from January to March between England, France, Ireland, Italy, Scotland and Wales. It began in 1883 as the Home Nations Championship between England, Ireland, Scotland and Wales, and then became the Five Nations Championship when France joined in 1910, and then the Six Nations Championship when Italy joined in 2000.

Spear Tackle: A dangerous tackle in which a player is picked up by a tackler and driven or dropped into the ground, often head, neck or shoulder first.

Springboks: Nickname of the South African rugby team.

Super Rugby: Annual competition between a total of 15 franchised professional clubs from Argentina (1), Australia (4), Japan (1), New Zealand (5) and South Africa (4).

Tackle: Physically stopping the ball carrier, and usually taking them to the ground.

Test: The name typically given for matches between two national teams. Also known as an international.

Tiers: World Rugby organises its member unions into three tiers. Tier 1 contains the elite standard teams who compete in the Rugby Championship and Six Nations Championship. Tier 2 is the next most senior level containing nations where rugby is established or growing quickly. Tier 3 contains nations where the game is developing.

Tight Five: The common name for the front row forwards and second row forwards together.

Tight-Head: The prop wearing the No.3 jersey, earning the name because his head in the scrum is between the opposition hooker and loose-head prop's shoulders. The tight-head prop is the anchor of the team's scrum.

Three-Quarters: Collective name for the centres and wingers in the backs.

Top 14: The senior level of professional club rugby in France made up of 14 teams.

Top League: The senior level of professional club rugby in Japan made up of 16 teams.

Touch: The out of bounds line which runs on either side of the pitch. Also known as the touchline.

Touch Rugby: A non-contact version of the game often played by children, as they begin to learn rugby, or adult recreational teams.

Try: A score of five points is awarded when the ball is carried or kicked across the try-line and touched down to the ground by an attacking player.

Try-Line: The line, extending across the pitch, behind which the ball must be placed to score a try.

Turnover: When a team gains possession of the ball from the other team from a set play (such as via a ruck), or in the loose (such as via a tackle).

22 Metre Drop-Out: The kick by the defending team to restart the match after a missed penalty or drop-goal, which goes out of bounds over the end goal-line, or is touched down by a defending player.

Union: The local, provincial or national organising and governing body for rugby competitions.

Up and Under: A tactical kick which is hit very high, but not very far, allowing the kicker and supporting players to easily run underneath and challenge to catch it. Also known as a Garry Owen, named after the Irish club where the tactic was first made popular.

Wallabies: Nickname of the Australian rugby team.

Welwitschias: Nickname of the Namibian rugby team.

Winger: Either of the two backs wearing the No.11 or No.14 jerseys. Often the fastest players, and the ones playing wide on the pitch, they also have an important role in defending and gathering deep kicks and starting counter-attacks.

World Rugby: Previously known as the International Rugby Football Board (IRFB) and then the International Rugby Board (IRB), World Rugby is the governing body of rugby in world.

Zinzan: A drop goal attempt, often by a forward from more than 40 metres, which only reaches two or three metres off the ground. Named after New Zealand legend Zinzan Brooke who famously performed this kick.

RUGBY WORLD CUP STATISTICS (1987-2015)

Champions: 3 – New Zealand; 2 – Australia, South Africa; 1 – England.

Runners-up: 3 - France; 2 – Australia, England; 1- New Zealand.

Third place: 2 - New Zealand, South Africa; 1 – Argentina, Australia, France, Wales.

Highest scores: 145 - New Zealand v Japan (Bloemfontein, 1995); 142 – Australia v Namibia (Adelaide, 2003); 111 – England v Uruguay (Brisbane, 2003).

Biggest winning margin: 142 – Australia v Namibia (Adelaide, 2003); 128 – New Zealand v Japan (Bloemfontein, 1995); 98 – England v Uruguay (Brisbane, 2003); 98 – New Zealand v Italy (Huddersfield, 1999).

Most points by a player in a match: 45 – Simon Culhane (New Zealand v Japan, 1995); 44 – Gavin Hastings (Scotland v Ivory Coast, 1995); 42 - Mat Rogers (Australia v Namibia, 2003).

Most points by a player in a tournament: 126 – Grant Fox (New Zealand, 1987); 113 – Jonny Wilkinson (England, 2003); 112 – Thierry Lacroix (France, 1995).

Most points by a player overall: 277 – Jonny Wilkinson (England, 1999, 2003, 2007, 2011); 227 - Gavin Hastings (Scotland, 1987, 1991, 1995); 195 – Michael Lynagh (Australia, 1987, 1991, 1995).

Most team points overall: 2,302 – New Zealand (50 matches); 1,545 – Australia (48 matches); 1,487 – France (48 matches); 1,379 – England (44 matches); 1,250 – South Africa (36 matches).

Most tries by a player in a match: 6 – Marc Ellis (New Zealand v Japan, 1995); 5 – Chris Latham (Australia v Namibia, 2003); 5 – Josh Lewsey (England v Uruguay, 1995).

Most tries by a player in a tournament: 8 – Jonah Lomu (New Zealand, 1999), Bryan Habana (South Africa, 2007), Julian Savea (New Zealand, 2015); 7 – Marc Ellis (New Zealand, 1995), Jonah Lomu (New Zealand, 1995), Doug Howlett (New Zealand, 2003), Mils Muliaina (New Zealand, 2003), Drew Mitchell (Australia, 2007).

Most tries by a player overall: 15, Jonah Lomu (New Zealand, 1995, 1999), Bryan Habana (South Africa, 2007, 2011, 2015); 14 – Drew Mitchell (Australia, 2007, 2011, 2015).

Most tries by a team in a match: 22 – Australia v Namibia (Adelaide, 2003); 21 – New Zealand v Japan (Bloemfontein, 1995).

Most tries by a team in a tournament: 52 – New Zealand (2007); 48 – New Zealand (2003); 43 – Australia (2003), New Zealand (1987); 41 – New Zealand (1995).

Most tries by a team overall: 311 – New Zealand (50 matches); 209 – Australia (48 matches); 171 – France (48 matches); 147 – England (44 matches); 141 – South Africa (36 matches).

Most penalty goals by a player in a tournament: 31 – Gonzalo Quesada (Argentina, 1999); 26 – Thierry Lacroix (France, 1995); 23 – Jonny Wilkinson (England, 2003), Handre Pollard (South Africa, 2015).

Most penalty goals by a player overall: 58 – Jonny Wilkinson (1999, 2003, 2007, 2011); 36 – Gavin Hastings (Scotland, 1987, 1991, 1995); 35 – Gonzalo Quesada (Argentina, 1999, 2003).

Most conversions by a player in a tournament: 30 – Grant Fox (New Zealand, 1987); 23 – Dan Carter (New Zealand, 2015); 22 – Percy Montgomery (South Africa, 2007).

Most conversions by a player overall: 58 – Dan Carter (New Zealand, 2003, 2007, 2011, 2015); 39 – Gavin Hastings (Scotland, 1987, 1991, 1995); 37 – Grant Fox (New Zealand, 1987, 1991); 36 – Michael Lynagh (Australia, 1987, 1991, 1995).

Most dropped goals by a player in a tournament: 8 – Jonny Wilkinson (England, 203); 6 – Jannie de Beer (South Africa, 1999), Gregor Townsend (Scotland, 1999).

Most dropped goals by a player overall: 14 – Jonny Wilkinson (England, 1999, 2003, 2007, 2011); 6 – Jannie de Beer (South Africa, 1999); 5 – Rob Andrew (England, 1987, 1991, 1995), Gareth Rees (Canada, 1987, 1991, 1995, 1999).

Most Rugby World Cup appearances by a player: 22 – Jason Leonard (England), Richie McCaw (New Zealand); 20 – Schalk Burger (South Africa), George Gregan (Australia), Keven Mealamu (New Zealand).

Most Rugby World Cup tournament appearances by a team: 8 – Argentina, Australia, Canada, England, France, Ireland, Italy, Japan, New Zealand, Romania, Scotland, South Africa, Wales; 7 – Fiji, Samoa, USA; 6 - Tonga; 5 – Namibia; 3 – Georgia; 2 – Uruguay, Zimbabwe; 1 – Ivory Coast, Portugal, Russia, Spain.

Players capped at Rugby World Cup for more than one country: Graeme Bachop (New Zealand 1991, 1995 & Japan 1999); France Bunce (Western Samoa 1991 & New Zealand 1995); Adrian Garvey (Zimbabwe 1991 & South Africa 1999); Jamie Joseph (New Zealand 1995 & Japan 1999); Dylan Mika (Western Samoa 1995 & New Zealand 1999); Matt Pini (Australia 1995 & Italy 1999); Ilivasi Tabua (Australia 1995 & Fiji 1999); Va'aiga Tuigamala (New Zealand 1991 & Samoa 1999).

REFERENCES

1. Rugby World Cup 2019, www.wikipedia.org/wiki/2019_Rugby_World_Cup

2. Rugby World Cup Hosts, www.wikipedia.org/wiki/Rugby_World_Cup_hosts

3. How Gareth Edwards' Wales inspired Japan's 2019 Rugby World Cup bid, www.walesonline.co.uk

4. Rugby World Cup 2015: The Official Tournament Guide, Carlton Books

5. Thirty Bullies: The History of the Rugby World Cup, written by Alison Kervin, Pocket Books

6. A Complete History of the Rugby World Cup: In Pursuit of Bill, written by Lance Peatey, New Holland Publishers

7. Japan to host 2019 tournament after officials approve revised proposal, written by Jamie Pandaram, www.dailytelegraph.com.au

8. Russia qualify for 2019 Rugby World Cup after Romania, Belgium and Spain sanctioned for ineligible players, written by Mitch Philips, www.independent.co.uk

9. Talking points from Rugby World Cup draw, written by Ben Coles, www.planetrugby.com

10. Way-to-early predictions for Rugby World Cup, written by ESPN staff, www.espn.com.au/rugby

11. List of international rugby teams, www.wikipedia.org/wiki/List_of_international_rugby_union_teams

12. The rise of the Tier 2 nations, written by Tousef Taclab, www.theroar.com.au

13. History of Japan, www wikipedia.org/wiki/History_of_Japan

14. 79 interesting facts about Japan, written by Jill Bartholomew, www.thefactretriever.com

15. Sport in Japan, www wikipedia.org/wiki/Sport_in_Japan

16. 2020 Summer Olympics, www wikipedia.org/wiki/2020_Summer_Olympics

17. Rugby Union in Japan, www wikipedia.org/wiki/Rugby_Union_in_Japan

18. Rugby in Japan, www.factsanddetails.com

19. Six Nations: Six players to watch, written by Louis Dore, www.inews.co.uk/sport,rugby-union

20. Six Nations Guide: Unofficial guide to the world's greatest rugby tournament, www.six-nations-guide.co.uk

21. Rassie: Scotland play like a Super Rugby side, www.sport24.co.za

22. A fan's guide to the Autumn test matches, www.autumninternationals.co.uk

23. These stereotypes perfectly sum up the style of rugby played in each country, www.intheloose.com

24. Manu coach in Samoa to begin RWC campaign, written by Thomas Airey, www.samoaobserver.ws

25. Samoa coach keen to build depth, written by Mariete Adams, www.sarugbymag.co.za

26. How Clive Woodward meeting changed Conor O'Shea's life, written by David Kelly, www.independent.ie

27. Italy at the Rugby World Cup, www.wikipedia.org/italy_at_the_rugby_world_cup

28. Chrysander Botha's hoping for home advantage at Exeter, by Neale Harvey, www.therugbypaper.co.uk

29. Namibia at the Rugby World Cup, www.wikipedia.org/namibia_at_the_rugby_world_cup

30. England at the Rugby World Cup, www.wikipedia.org/england_at_the_rugby_world_cup

31. France at the Rugby World Cup, www.wikipedia.org/france_at_the_rugby_world_cup

32. Tonga at the Rugby World Cup, www.wikipedia.org/namibia_at_the_rugby_world_cup

33. They don't want us to be competitive, by Paul Cully, www. stuff.co.nz

34. Why Georgia has rugby on its mind ahead of this year's World Cup, written by George Ramsey, www.edition-m.cnn.com

35. Georgia national rugby union team, www.wikipedia.org

36. Fijian rugby on an upward curve, by Cian Tracey, www. independent.ie

37. Rugby World Cup 2003: The definitive guide, The Guardian

38. Essential Rugby, written by Neil Armstrong, Paragon Publishing Ltd

39. Rugby skills, tactics and Rules, written by Tony Williams & John McKittrick, Bloomsbury Publishing

40. Rugby Union: The official guide to playing the game, written by Howard Johnson, Haynes Publishing

41. Rugby World Cup boss planning for typhoons and quakes in disaster-prone Japan, www.the42.ie/rugby

42. Extensive contingencies drawn up for Rugby World Cup 2019, written by Duncan Bech, www.spoer360.com

43. World Rugby pondering emerging nations as RWC hosts, www.sport24.co.za

44. The future of rugby: an HSBC report, by The Futures Company

CREDITS

Cover and interior design: Annika Naas

Layout: Amnet

Cover photos and figure: © AdobeStock

Interior figures: © AdobeStock

Managing editor: Elizabeth Evans

Copyeditor: Qurratulain Zaheer

TOKYO STADIUM, CHOFU
(OPENED 2001, CAPACITY: 49,970)

 INTERNATIONAL STADIUM YOKOHAMA, OKOHAMA
(OPENED 1998, CAPACITY: 72,327)

 SHIZUOKA STADIUM ECOPA, FUKUROI
(OPENED 2001, CAPACITY: 50,889)

 HANAZONO RUGBY STADIUM, HIGASHIOSAKA
(OPENED 1929, CAPACITY: 30,000)

 CITY OF TOYOTA STADIUM, TOYOTA
(OPENED 2001, CAPACITY: 45,000)

 OITA STADIUM, OITA
(OPENED 2001, CAPACITY: 40,000)

 KAMAISHI RECOVERY MEMORIAL STADIUM, KAMAISHI
(OPENED 2018, CAPACITY: 16,187)

 KUMAGAYA RUGBY STADIUM, KUMAGAYA
(OPENED 1991, CAPACITY: 30,000)

 KOBE MISAKI STADIUM, KOBE
(OPENED 2001, CAPACITY: 30,132)

 KUMAMOTO STADIUM, KUMAMOTA
(OPENED 1998, CAPACITY: 32,000)

 SAPPORO DOME, SAPPORO
(OPENED 2001, CAPACITY: 41,410)

 FUKUOKA HAKATANOMORI STADIUM, FUKUOKA
(OPENED 1995, CAPACITY: 22,563)

THE VENUES

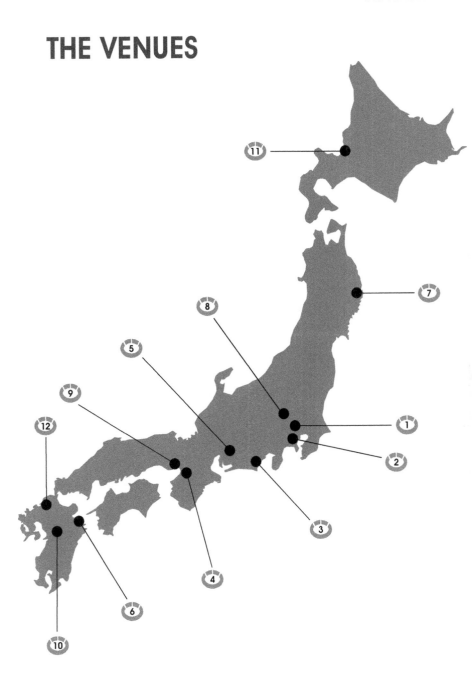

KNOCKOUT STAGE

Quarter-finals

QF No.1
Winner of Pool C v Runner-up of Pool D
Saturday, October 19 at Oita Stadium, ko 4.15pm (GMT 7.15am)

QF No.2
Winner of Pool B v Runner-up of Pool A
Saturday, October 19 at Tokyo Stadium, ko 7.15pm (GMT 10.15am)

QF No.3
Winner of Pool D v Runner-up of Pool C
Sunday, October 20 at Oita Stadium, ko 4.15pm (GMT 7.15)

QF No.4
Winner of Pool A v Runner-up of Pool B
Sunday, October 20 at Tokyo Stadium, ko 7.15pm (GMT 10.15am)

Semi-finals

SF No.1
Winner of QF No.1 v Winner of QF No.2
Saturday, October 26 at International Stadium Yokohama, ko 5.00pm (GMT 8.00am)

SF No.2
Winner of QF No.3 v Winner of QF No.4
Sunday, October 27 at International Stadium Yokohama, ko 6.00pm (GMT 9.00am)

Bronze medal match

Loser of SF No.1 v Loser of SF No.2
Friday, November 1 at Tokyo Stadium, ko 6.00pm (GMT 9.00am)

Final

Winner of SF No.1 v Winner of SF No.2
Saturday, November 2 at International Stadium Yokohama, ko 6.00pm (GMT 9.00am)

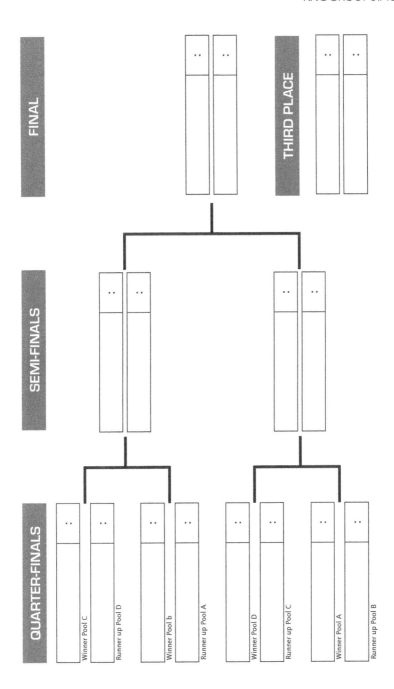

CHECK OUT THESE GREAT BOOKS

168 p., b/w,
paperback,
5.5˝ x 8.5˝
ISBN: 9781782551751
$ 14.95 US

Shane Stay

EUROPEAN SOCCER LEAGUES 2019

EVERYTHING YOU NEED TO KNOW ABOUT THE 2019/20 SEASON

This book gives every fan an all-access look into Europe's famous club teams, including the players, coaches, each team's style of play, their future direction, along with background on key stadiums and cities. The reader will find information on the most famous European leagues: the Premiere League, Serie A, La Liga, and Bundesliga. They have been the leaders in world club soccer for decades. This book takes the fan through every aspect of the upcoming club season, illuminating the very best of European soccer.

FROM MEYER & MEYER SPORT

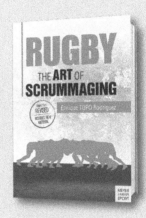

Enrique TOPO Rodriquez

RUGBY: THE ART OF SCUMMAGING

A HISTORY, A MANUAL AND A LAW
DISSERTATION ON THE RUGBY SCRUM

This book is one of the most comprehensive rugby scrum theses ever since the inception of the rugby union. It will allow coaches to develop players who understand the skills, thereby increasing their efficiency and making the scrum safer. Covering every aspect from history, technique, safety, and physical conditioning to scrum law, it is the perfect coaching tool for teachers and coaches of all levels.

376 p., b/w, 45 photos,
paperback,
6.5" x 9.5"
ISBN: 9781782551553
$ 24.95 US

MEYER & MEYER Sport
Von-Coels-Str. 390
52080 Aachen
Germany

Phone   +49 02 41 - 9 58 10 - 13
Fax   +49 02 41 - 9 58 10 - 10
E-Mail   sales@m-m-sports.com
Website   www.m-m-sports.com

All books available as E-books.

MEYER
& MEYER
SPORT